CIVIL AND SAVAGE

ENCOUNTERS

THE WORLDLY TRAVEL LETTERS OF AN
IMPERIAL RUSSIAN NAVY OFFICER
1860–1861

PAVEL N. GOLOVIN

TRANSLATED AND ANNOTATED

BY

BASIL DMYTRYSHYN

AND

E.A.P. CROWNHART-VAUGHAN

INTRODUCTION BY

THOMAS VAUGHAN

PORTLAND

WESTERN IMPRINTS
THE PRESS OF THE OREGON HISTORICAL SOCIETY
MCMLXXXIII

Library of Congress Cataloging in Publication Data:

Golovin, Pavel Nikolaevich, 1823-1862.
    Civil and savage encounters.

    (North Pacific studies; 5)
    Translated from Russian.
    Appeared in 1863 in the Russian magazine, "Morskoi Sbornik."
    Includes index.
    1. Alaska—Description and travel—To 1867.
2. Voyages to the Pacific coast.
3. Russians—Alaska—History.   4. Europe—Description and travel—1800-1918.   5. Golovin, Pavel Nikolaevich, 1823-1862.   I. Morskoi sbornik.   II. Title.   III. Series.
F907.G63 1982   910.4   82-22487
ISBN 0-87595-067-1
ISBN 0-87595-095-7 (pbk.)

Printed in the United States of America.

Production of this volume was supported in part by funds provided by the S. S. Johnson Foundation and the Northwest Area Foundation.

To a great Tlingit scholar,
the late Erna Vladimirovna Siebert
Institute of Ethnography, Academy of Sciences
Leningrad

Мы помним чудное мгновенье,
Передо нами явилась ты . . .
Как гений чистой красоты.

We recall that wondrous moment
When before us you appeared . . .
Like the spirit of pure beauty.
(After A. Pushkin, "To . . ." [1825])

NORTH PACIFIC STUDIES SERIES

CONTENTS

ILLUSTRATIONS

All specially drawn for this volume by Karen Beyers.

PREFACE

This is volume five in the Oregon Historical Society's North Pacific Studies Series. It is a companion publication to the fourth volume in that series, *The End of Russian America: Captain P. N. Golovin's Last Report, 1862* (Oregon Historical Society, 1979), a translation of Captain Golovin's official report to the Imperial Russian government on the condition of Russia's American colonies. By contrast the present volume, Golovin's personal correspondence to his St. Petersburg family during his trip to Russian America, provides broad impressions of Europe, the eastern seabord, Panama. Acapulco and San Francisco, as well as the fogbound outposts of Russian America.

Although the letters were not intended for publication, Golovin's untimely death so shocked his friends and family that his mother consented to release the letters to the editors of the official periodical of the Russian Navy, *Morskoi Sbornik* (Naval Anthology). This highly regarded journal published maritime history and literature as well as notices and reports and featured the letters in 1863 as "From the Travel Letters of P. N. Golovin" (vol. 66).

Our goal in translation is to be completely accurate, and particularly in a work such as this to use the English language with the same flare, grace and style with which the author used the Russian language. Golovin's personality is very much revealed in the intimacy of these letters and we have striven to preserve his humor, affection, sly wit and masterful and rich use of the language to burnish this translation. We use the Library of Congress system of translation but omit ligatures and apostrophes. We retain Golovin's use of French. We use contemporary spelling of place names for the convenience of the reader (Sitka and Kodiak for Sitkha and Kadiak). Golovin often used initials to refer to persons familiar to his mother and sister; we have identified these persons wherever possible. The author used dual dates on his letters; at that time Russia still used the Julian calendar, which was twelve days behind the Gregorian calendar used in the West. (In this text the Julian date precedes the Gregorian.)

In this as in all our projects involving Russian source materials we have had superb scholarly cooperation from colleagues and institutions in North America and in the USSR. We particularly wish to thank the following: The Geographical Society of the Academy of Sciences, Leningrad: A. F. Treshnikov and the late M. I. Belov; Saltykov-Shchedrin State Public Library, Leningrad; Central Naval Museum, Leningrad: E. G. Kushnarev; Museum of Anthropology and Ethnography of the Academy of Sciences, Leningrad: R. V. Kinzhalov, the late E. V. Siebert, R. G. Liapunova, A. D. Dridzo and G. Dzeniskevich; Lenin Library, Moscow: B. P. Kanevskii; Institute of Ethnography of the Academy of Sciences, Moscow: Academician Iu. V. Bromlei, S. G. Fedorova; Institute of General History of the Academy of Sciences, Moscow: N. N. Bolkhovitinov; Zhdanov State University Library, Irkutsk; Geographical Society, Far Eastern Sector, Khabarovsk. In Alaska, the Right Reverend Gregory, Russian Orthodox Bishop of Sitka and Alaska. In Canada, James R. Gibson of York University, Toronto. In Washington DC, Robert V. Allen of the Library of Congress. In Portland, Colonel M. J. Poniatowski-d'Ermengard. Colleagues associated with the Oregon Historical Society who have assisted this publication in so many ways: Thomas Vaughan, Director and General Editor of North Pacific Studies Series; Priscilla Knuth, Executive Editor of the

Oregon Historical Quarterly; Bruce Hamilton, Executive Editor of Publications: Karen Beyers, who prepared the original illustrations for this volume; James B. Thayer, Chairman, Publications Committee.

The Northwest Area Foundation of St. Paul, Minnesota and the S. S. Johnson Foundation under Samuel S. Johnson and Elizabeth Hill Johnson have given significant subventions to the publication of this volume. The entire program of the retrieval, translation and publication of Russian source materials has been inspired and supported by the North Pacific (Irkutsk Archival) Research Group of the Oregon Historical society whose bold chairmen have been John Youell, Samuel S. Johnson and presently Jane West Youell.

To all who have so generously aided this international scholarly venture we are indeed indebted.

Basil Dmytryshyn
E.A.P. Crownhart-Vaughan
Portland, 1982

INTRODUCTION

In 1968 my wife E. A. P. Crownhart-Vaughan and I completed our first cross-country research linkup in the Soviet Union and took the train up to Finland. There we spent 10 days working in the magnificent Russian archives located in Helsinki—or perhaps one should say *under* that once imperial capital of the Grand Duchy of Finland. The enormous research stacks seem to run for blocks beneath the university buildings established in the center of this storied old Baltic port. As part of our decompression we swam in the Gulf of Finland on sunny afternoons, just a short excursion ride from the downtown docks.

One hot August afternoon we stroked through the blue bay waters surrounding the vast sea fortress of Sveaborg, the "Gibraltar of the North," an immense rock and walled pile which screened the western approaches to old Helsingfors. Floating in the bright sunshine we regarded the typically "mud yellow" and dun-colored fortifications squatting on acres of granite. We were in the approximate anchorage from which Victoria's favorite, Charles Napier, and Admiral Parseval-Deschênes, with the majestic Anglo-French flotilla, made their inglorious reconnaissance of the defense works during the first summer of the Crimean War in 1854. We tend to forget the far-flung engagements of that seemingly localized war. Vice Admiral Napier retired to Kiel, but the following summer their equally ill-starred replacements from

Sevastopol arrived. The mortars of Dundas and Penaud pulverized much of Sveaborg, and they also suceeded in igniting a huge stockpile of pitch earlier purchased by British naval suppliers, who had long depended on the Scandinavian forests to maintain their global naval supremacy.

I suppose that we recalled the last maneuvers of the powerful but ill-prepared Baltic Fleet which Admiral Zinovii Rozhestvenskii gathered from Kronstadt, Helsingfors and Reval. Thirty-seven ships sailed from the Baltic under his command in 1903, off to a Japanese rendezvous at Tsushima and annihilation. Fifteen years later elements of a significant Russian fleet were stationed here in World War I, often locked in the winter ice.

But now it was summer and we struck for shore to clamber up the fallen blocks and lonely battlements. We soon penetrated the silent inner works, the eerie magazine and gun rooms. Filtered light filled the chapel, assembly and mess rooms. It was lonely but magnificent, a geometrically conceived granite giant, impregnable and solid enough to please Vauban himself.

Then there was the brooding officers' mess, with little to evoke boisterous times past. The dank and shadowy remnants of a solid era did not then reveal that my swimming partner would a few summers later turn up in Moscow a dusty file related to Sveaborg. She would be allowed to breathe life back into a most vibrant man, a Russian sailor whose songs and verses filled these lively rooms before the Crimean War. I realize now that he may have been lurking about on the warm summer breeze that day, hoping to be noticed.

The editors of this letter book, Basil Dmytryshyn and E. A. P. Crownhart-Vaughan pointed out in Pavel N. Golovin's *The End of Russian America* (OHS, 1979) that little is known about Golovin's too short life. His father was from the Kursk gubernia, a fertile black-earth administrative district a few hundred miles south of Moscow. His family were emphatically of the ruling class. The noble Golovins first achieved fame in the 17th century through Petr Petrovich Golovin who died in 1645. Field Marshal General Admiral Fedor Alekseevich Golovin was made a count of the Holy

Roman Empire by Leopold I in 1701. Privy Counselor Nikolai A. Golovin became a gentleman-in-waiting to Tsaritsa Elizabeth Petrovna, and, as recorded, the first freemason among the Russian aristocracy. His son Nikolai Nikolaevich (1759-1821), father of Pavel Nikolaevich, was a senator and a member of the Council.

The spare record suggests that Golovin's father died just before Pavel's birth in 1822, and that his mother never remarried. She remained in St. Petersburg but often traveled to family estates near Reval (Tallin) in Estonia. (This was and still is a favored Russian summer seaside resort.) At the age of eight Pavel Nikolaevich Golovin was enrolled in the Aleksandrovskii Military Academy, also in the capital. On 7 January 1837 he was promoted naval cadet. Later that year and in 1838 he was cruising in the Baltic on the frigates *Proserpine* and *Imperator Peter I*. On 21 December 1838 he was promoted to midshipman. In 1839 he sailed to North Germany from Kronstadt on the *Melpomena* as well as in the gulfs of Finland and Riga. The year 1840 saw an arctic voyage from the base at Archangel around the northern capes to the Baltic and Kronstadt, the water-girded fortress guarding St. Petersburg. During 1841-45 Golovin cruised the Baltic and North seas in the *LeFort*, and was promoted to lieutenant in 1844. In 1846 he sailed the transport *Abo* to Naples and then back to Kronstadt, a significant command experience.

From 1847 to 1853 Golovin served either ashore at Reval and Sveaborg or on the *LeFort* and steamers *Neva* and *Smelii*, the *Prokhor* and *Emgeiten* and the frigate *Amfitrid*. It is interesting to note, as our Russian colleague and naval historian Evgenii Grigorevich Kushnarev has informed us, that Golovin served on the *Smelii* and the *Emgeiten* as flag officer to the famous Russian admiral and circumnavigator Bellingshausen, who with many other Russian cadets had received his formative training in the much-admired British navy. On 31 March 1853, Golovin was promoted Captain-Lieutenant and sent far south to command the port at Astrakhan. He was then about 30 years old. An important development was his advancement as senior adjutant in the Inspector's Department of the Naval Ministry. As a result of this career assignment he produced a serious analysis for the official naval publication *Morskoi Sbornik* (*Naval Anthology*) entitled "Some Thoughts Concerning the Responsibilities of Senior Officers on Ships." He was much troubled by the inhumane treatment of seamen, such as punishment by flogging (known in Russia as knouting). His concern would fit with other reforms then under review throughout the Russian bureaucracy.

Although he served with distinction during the Crimean War there is as yet no striking detail. We do know that in 1860, as talent and privilege combined, he was appointed an imperial chamberlain, a position of immense social and political power. He was ready for the most far-reaching assignments.

But let us return to those early years, those days which an acquaintance referred to in his obituary as the zesty period of *kipiatok krovi* the "boiling of the blood."

Voin Andreevich Rimskii-Korsakov (elder brother of the composer and later a rear admiral) wrote of Golovin, his closest friend, in an introduction to these intimate letters to his mother and sisters:

> In 1844 I was ill and was assigned ashore to spend the winter at Sveaborg with the 25th squadron and arrived late in the fall. P. N. [Golovin] was at that time assigned to the 26th squadron, and was spending his second consecutive winter at Sveaborg . . . . There was no space to be found for me in the new wing . . . so I immediately arranged to be placed next to P. N., and since our two rooms had a common door, this made a very pleasant apartment for us. We made one of the rooms into a bedroom and study, and received guests in the other room.

Rimskii-Korsakov goes on to say:

> Another bit of good news was that the officers of the 26th had a common table. This was established through P. N.'s initiative and thoughtfulness . . . . Once he conceived the idea, he undertook all the work himself, which is to say that he assumed the role of host. The table was always well set; there were three courses at dinner, and at least one at supper.

And all of this was accomplished at a tremendous bargain—it cost each of us only 12 or 13 rubles per month, and that included meals for our batmen. Each man provided his own tea. There were seven or eight of us, all bachelors, who were part of this arrangement. The oldest was no more than 25. P. N. and I were senior in service, having graduated together. P. N. was then senior lieutenant on the *LeFort*. The personalities in our group were extremely varied, as well as the education, attitudes and background, but I found them bound together in a light-hearted friendly little group. Of course not all of the officers of the 26th were invited to be part of the common table. There were two who were such trumps no one wanted to lead them. They were even relegated to the upper story.

We would gather together for dinner at the appointed hour, and immediately afterward we would sit down for an entire hour playing cards for small stakes. The game had its own purpose in that the winner did not receive anything—all of the winnings, no matter whose or how much, went into a common fund which was under P. N.'s supervision. When we had accumulated 25-30 rubles in this fund, we would choose an appropriate day, rent a big sleigh, squeeze everyone in our group into it, and go romping off to Helsingfors [over the frozen bay] where we would celebrate with a night on the town. Our revelry would be arranged for dinner or supper in one of the best hotels in Helsingfors, but sometimes our fund was not enough to cover the cost of all the champagne we consumed . . . . I must say that more than once such revelry gave birth to riotous times. Sometimes even university students, who were usually rather unfriendly in observing our officers and our enthusiastic jollity, would join in with us. We must remember that Finland, an imperial Grand Duchy since 1810, was in effect an occupied country, and much of the Swedish population as well as the Finnish would have been inhospitable.

Many times, however, our group had quite a different kind of good time. For example we often went on outings together as a company around Sveaborg, but not as everyone else strolled; we went along the rooftops and walls or along the rocky ledges above the shore, especially the latter, when there was a stiff wind and the surf was breaking. In leaping from these obstacles there were many amusing moments, particularly with those who were not gifted with dexterity. We all loved to sing together in our own little chorus, and after supper we would not only sing all kinds of songs, but often we even entertained our acquaintances with serenades on the streets. P. N. in particular had memorized a huge repertoire of all kinds of songs, and he was very quick at composing verses. He would not only write the verse for choral and drinking songs, he would compose the music for them as well, and several of these songs became traditional among the officers. Only last year (1861) I heard a cadet singing one of them, a serenade.

Boiling of the blood indeed! Obviously a rolling boil. And yet at the same time Golovin was imbued with a dedication to hard work and a sense of the responsibilities of command. Life was often hard in the fleet at sea or ashore—the rigor of Baltic winters alone would have taxed the strongest. But as Rimskii-Korsakov points out: "In many ways P. N. provided a feeling of good humor. He was something of a tuning fork for us." One has the feeling of Golovin having a special part of Russian character, perhaps one of Tolstoy's attractive people. "Only his equable personality, and the tact with which he was gifted could provide the means of bringing together into one unified family so many individual personalities without resorting to duplicity or an ingratiating manner." How interesting to find this merry nature, combined with the diplomatic finesse and grave introspections revealed in his letters.

We also know that in 1850 he and Rimskii-Korsakov translated work of the Jurien de la Gravière family. It is possible some of this work was done at Reval and Sveaborg since they spent long months together at these outposts. Their two-volume translation concerning French naval warfare during the Republic and Empire was published in 1851 by the Naval Academic Committee. The work appeared without mention of the names of the translators. In the midst of that great era of literary output, Russian periodicals gave it excellent notice, judging it one of the finest books published in the Russian language in 1851. During the same year *Morskoi Sbornik* published Golovin's translation of the battle between the French frigate *Surveillance* and the British *Quebec*, which blew up during the action in 1799. This publication was followed by his translation of the expedition of Count d'Estre in the Antilles. An article in memory of Peter the Great on the shores of Lake Pleshcheev was followed by another translation from the French of an essay on the life of the renowned French admiral, Turville. By convention these skillful pieces were only initialed, and their quality attracted curious inquiry among a social class much given to reading and winter-bound salon discussions. One would doubt that the secret was kept long.

What must we think today of this exuberant sailor from Kursk and St. Petersburg who traveled and served from the grandeur of the Caucasus to the northern bays, the length of the Baltic and down to Naples? He speaks or has familiarity with at least four languages. We know that he is a creature of privilege, but one infused with a fine sense of patriotism and noblesse oblige. There is a certain sense of attitude and knowledge of old dreams, some sense perhaps of the memories and desires awakened by the Russian army officers who in 1813 entered Europe and then the gates of Paris with the victorious Tsar Alexander I, another dreamer. While it is unsaid, one can supposed that Pavel Golovin, who had more than a casual sense of history, was well aware of the astute Marquis de Custine's gallic observation about favored Russian travelers allowed out of the borders who laughed all the way to Paris and cried all the way home. With an elegant standard of deportment and class Golovin was not about to brood over his fate in a Lermontov manner, but he does make many comparisons, often wry ones. Yet he knows very well who he is and how he ought to function. Admiral-General Grand Duke Constantine and his naval colleagues would otherwise never have charged him with so important and delicate an assignment as the

Alaskan investigation. He could not have risen in effect from a competent and reliable government inspector to a tactical player in the final determinations about the sale of Alaska, which is precisely how he functioned in the last year of his too short life. As we know, his direct superior, Constantine, head of the State Council, opposed the renewal of the Russian American Company charter, and he was, let us remember, the Tsar's brother and adviser. Golovin on assignment was skirting close to the throne.

Rimskii-Korsakov remarks in his introduction that these informal family letters were never intended for publication. This also provides us with clearer, more useful insights into a constrained society and atmosphere as we compare (as does his friend) Golovin's private letters from Sitka with his important official report on the state of the Russian American Company in Alaska. We are provided long-submerged insights on a broad and cosmopolitan level which must be considered remarkable if not unique.

The intimate views afforded begin with Golovin's first letter home from his global journey and reveal an astute observer in a mise en scène one could scarcely hope would come to light. A highly trained and civilized military officer slips his professional restraints while writing home, yielding a string of solid nuggets concerning life in the mid-nineteenth century outside Russia feverishly viewed for the first time. Golovin travels to Berlin, Dresden, Leipzig, Hamburg, Wiesbaden, et cetera, to Paris and its Palais Royale, Notre Dame, the Bal Mabille pleasure garden, soot-covered London, bustling Liverpool, the high seas, the Tremont House in Boston, the palatial Fifth Avenue Hotel in New York. Charles Dickens, Thackeray and Martineau come to mind and he in every way equals and often exceeds their skills. Washington, Panama, Acapulco, the exotic scenes of San Francisco and Sitka are sharply sketched. And certainly by indirection, in what is left unsaid or hinted at, important aspects of Russian life and attitudes in the reign of Alexander II are revealed. And much is personally painful to him and to his pride: "People on the street are well behaved, and quiet and sober."

He is not showing off for his family at home as he meticulously reports most of his adventures across Prussia, France, England and the North Atlantic.

His views on operatic production and vocal deportment are easy and informed. *I Puritani* is obviously an old familiar. And he is hardly the first Russian to approach the gaming tables in a German spa, but he may be the first to count the steps. He luxuriates in the sights of Paris, but never mentions the recent humiliation of Russian arms in the dislocative Crimean War. He simply states that London is covered with soot. How interesting his description of North Atlantic passenger life and the sometimes amusing and droll habits of Boston and New York. Europeans it appears will never tire of describing American eating habits.

Among other expressions which enrich these pages is his belief in a sense of progress and that the next generation will not have so many problems. His views, while perhaps not uniformly accurate, are intelligently made, whether it be about a locomotive cow-catching grill, Patti's singing, or the occasional splendor of American hotels (such as the Fifth Avenue in New York), steamboats and railroads. He loves the cow-catching grill.

Golovin treats the problems of Russian serfdom versus American slavery and the freedom of public conversations versus the silence of Russian travelers intrigues. He observes street behavior in Hamburg; "there is no shouting here, no running about, no pushing, no offers of services and arguments about pay." He relishes civility and a sense of order. Is he shocked by the grime of London, or perhaps relieved? He is amazed at the broad streets and the large number of carriages in America. He sees his first sewing machine in San Francisco, and naturally describes it to maman and his sister. In Sitka there are no carriages and few cattle or horses, but a rocky and brooding bay nearby reminds him of *Der Freischutz*. His romantic nature often surfaces.

He is not wholly in accord with the Russian American Company "which looks so good on paper," but appears to be living in a dream world. But he is keen on the once brave and warlike Aleuts, despite their excessess, and much impressed by the Kolosh

(Tlingit) who obviously control the land outside the walls of Sitka. The fierce, unconquerable Kolosh tribesmen carry their own revolvers and muskets, and can only be cowed by a 24-hour display of Russian artillery (The Company trains its cannon directly upon their restive village next to New Arkhangel). When Golovin states it, one accepts the fact that the Kolosh sold Indian slaves to the Russians. It is he who says Russians need always to hold important Kolosh tribesmen hostage, as part of the ongoing relationship, a Russian practice employed during the conquest of Siberia and the Aleutian chain, and elsewhere.

Throughout his long and sometimes vexing journey across half the world Golovin really never loses his sparkle and humor and good health, except that the screaming of unsupervised children he encounters on trains and small ships drives him to a rage. Most understandable. His views on Alaska and the offshore islands are useful in our considerations today. One can only regret that his original design to return home through Kamchatka was not carried out. His letters across Siberia would surely have been eye-openers. As it was, his reasons for returning through Washington take on much meaning, for it did most distinctly involve a substantial change of travel plan.

In New Arkhangel one is provided unique views of the levels and degrees of existence operating in the colony, reminiscent perhaps of stratification at home; great tensions, boredom and ennui abound, born of precisely delineated behavior in the extremes, with not much activity in the broad middle ground. But wherever he is and whomever he sees, Pavel Nikolaevich seems well favored and approachable, attracting to his person people from every walk of life. No portrait or photograph has been found to date, but through his friends one is reminded somehow of an earlier spirit of enlightenment. Certainly he must have seemed to many a *beau ideal*, the finished and compassionate gentleman to the braided tips of his epaulets. Such a swath he and his colleague Sergei Kostlivtsov must have cut through the cramped rooms of the Russian American Company's enfogged rulers. What dreams some mothers must have had, and not only for their daughters.

When he left St. Petersburg in July 1860, Golovin's naval superiors ordered him to stop in Washington for a briefing by Baron de Stoeckl, the well-established and well-regarded Russian ambassador to President James Buchanan. From there he was to move on by water to Panama, take the Chagres crossing and proceed up to Acapulco, San Francisco and Sitka. Upon completing his assignment he was to return to St. Petersburg via Kamchatka and Siberia. As we shall see he could not get back to envoy Stoeckl fast enough with his views on Alaska. Oh, to have been a fly on the wall, or better yet a bug, to have heard their exchange of ideas. His enigmatic entry, "the journey to Washington ended successfully" hardly satisfies. His comments about Stoeckl and his acerbic remarks about the wartime capital being infested with "riffraff" will naturally intrigue the reader.

To his mother and sister with whom he has earlier communicated in a six-week delivery via the newly established Pony Express, he writes: "We had dinner with Stoeckl twice, and he came to spend three hours with us. During these meetings we completed all our business with him. He is in complete agreement with our ideas and will write accordingly to the Grand Duke [Constantine, opponent of renewing the Russian American Company charter] and to Prince Gorchakov." Well, who is to say? Golovin obviously did play a persuasive role, but what it was, we cannot presently evaluate. Stoeckl would certainly have been impressed by him and by his several high-born connections. He may have welcomed and perhaps approved the ideas of Golovin and Kostlivtsov.

Golovin's official report is given in full in the companion volume, *The End of Russian America: Captain P . N . Golovin's Last Report, 1862* (Oregon Historical Society, 1979). His recommendations were aimed at putting Russian American on a sound economic basis, offering protection to the native and creole population, and dismantling much of the burdensome bureaucracy that already pervaded Russian America. His findings were referred to a fourteen-man investigative committee composed of government officials, scientists and Company officers. Their exhaustive report was published in two volumes in St. Petersburg in 1863 by the Department of Foreign Commerce. A translation of this work, *Doklad Komiteta ob ustroistve Russkikh Amerikanskikh kolonii* [Report of the Committee on the Organization of the American Colonies], will be published as part of this series, North Pacific Studies.

We can see what an interesting and productive human being Pavel Nikolaevich Golovin was, exhibiting all that is best in the Russian character. How troubling it is to learn that soon after he returned to St. Petersburg in August of 1861 he accepted another assignment, fell ill and died. Perhaps he dined out too often. Perhaps our ardent traveler was not so well as he thought. And perhaps the rigors of his stay in Russian American and his travels were greater than he realized. As Rimskii-Korsakov later eulogized: "He loved to talk about his adventures, and everyone loved to listen to him tell tales of the sea and of his voyages . . . . He got along with everyone . . . Such a man was a rare treasure."

In January 1862 he undertook the inspection of a garrison battalion where he found himself inadequately dressed for the harsh weather. It seems a bit strange that this detachment was on "indefinite leave." The "inquiry" was made in unheated barracks in the bitter cold of January. Golovin was certainly no stranger to arctic weather, but he was suffering from a liver complication. Then, although he was already seriously ill he was sent on to Hamburg where his condition rapidly deteriorated. He managed to finish his assignment, but upon returning to St. Petersburg was so weak he could scarcely stumble up the steps of his house and ring for help. Captain Golovin was carried to his bed. Three days later he died of pneumonia and complications.

And so, in the words of one of his own verses from his hotblooded days, and much too soon for Pavel Nikolaevich and for us, "Mother Sea carried him back to his native shore."

Thomas Vaughan, Executive Director
Oregon Historical Society

CIVIL AND SAVAGE

ENCOUNTERS

Berlin   4/16 July 1860[*]

Here I am in Berlin. On Thursday, June 30, I made final
preparations for my journey. There was so much to do and so much
running about that my feet ached, and I still did not manage to do
everything, nor to say goodbye to everyone. The morning of our
departure Brt. and Glch. came to see me, and at 1:00 PM I left
home with Glch., who took me to the steamship. Dn. and Vn.[†]
were there too. At precisely 2:00 PM we left Peterburg [St.
Petersburg] aboard the streamer *Peterhof*, because the *Neva*, on
which we were to sail to Stettin, was anchored at Kronshtadt.
Along the way we had dinner, or rather I was invited to dine with
Kostlivtsov,[‡] who was accompanied by his entire family. At 4:00
we were transferred to the *Neva*, and at 4:45 we raised anchor and
started on our voyage.

At 5:00 AM Sunday we reached Swinemünde. Customs officials
immediately came on board to inspect our baggage, while the ship
sailed on to Stettin, where we docked at 8:30 am. In all fairness to
the Prussian customs officials, they scarcely looked at our

---

[*]Throughout, Golovin uses both Russian (Julian) and Western (Gregorian) dates.—Eds.
[†]Voin Andreevich Rimskii-Korsakov (1822-1871), Russian hydrographer and longtime close friend
of Golovin, later rear Admiral. In 1852-55, he explored and mapped the lower Amur region. His
brother was the composer Nikolai Andreevich Rimskii-Korsakov, author of the introduction to
these letters as published in *Morskoi Sbornik*.—Eds.
[‡]Acting State Councillor Sergei Kostlivtsov, appointed by the Ministry of Finance to accompany
Golovin on his investigative mission to Russian America.—Eds.

baggage, and took our word that we were not carrying any contraband. From the ship we went to the railroad station, left our luggage, and bought our train tickets. Since the train was not due to leave until 2:00 pm, we took this opportunity to look around the city. Stettin is not a large town, but it is clean and nicely laid out. There are soldiers everywhere, and from a distance we saw that they were changing the guard in the square, but we did not go to watch because this takes place frequently, as at home.

At 2:00 we left for Berlin. The train is beautiful. The second class cars are precisely like our first class cars on the Peterhof Line. The distance is 17 miles, which is about 120 *versts*, and the cost is 3 *thalers*, or slightly less than 3 silver rubles. The train stops several times, but only for three minutes, during which time women come up to the cars with fruit, beer, lemonade, cakes, bread, et cetera. The way is not particularly picturesque, but everywhere one sees cultivated fields and groves of trees, all beautifully kept up. There is evidence of diligent work every-where, and not a plot of land goes to waste.

By 6:00 PM we were in Berlin. We handed over our baggage checks at the station, announced that we would be staying at the Hôtel de Rome, went to the hotel by carriage, and an hour later our bags were delivered to us. Our hotel is located on the best street, the *Unter den Linden*. It is a wide shady boulevard, and carriages drive along both sides. All the homes are clean and comfortable . . . carriages drive to and fro. We took rooms on the lower floor, with windows opening onto the street. Our rooms are lovely. The sitting room has three windows, and next to it is a bedroom with two windows and two beds, with all appurtenances. For this we pay three thalers a day. The hotel has all conveniences, and baths and both hot and cold water. Of course we could have had less expensive rooms, but they would have been high up, with windows on the court, and we wanted to be able to see what was happening on the street, and not have to go up all the stairs to the third floor. Here we are only two steps from the street.

After we had changed our clothes and dined, we took a *fiacre* and went to the Royal Gardens. This is something like our Islere, but with a great difference: the entrance fee is 30 silver kopecks. One enters through gates, and on the right there is a marvelous room with a stage. Every day there is either a concert or a theatrical performance. From this room one proceeds into a lovely shady garden, which is illuminated with gas lights. Above the fountains there are revolving gas lights like the one that illuminated the English store [in St. Petersburg] during the coronation [of Alexander II]. Similar stars, circles and other shapes are scattered all through the walkways, and it is as light as day. There are throngs of ladies with their children, and men sit at little tables and listen to the fine orchestra and drink beer or eat ice cream. Everyone is as lively as can be, but they are all well behaved. One does not see drunkeness or brawling. At 11:00 PM everything closes up, the gas is turned off, and everyone goes home. We met almost all of our fellow passengers from the ship in the Royal Gardens, drank wine with them, and went home together.

Today I arose at 7:00. There was already a good deal of activity on the streets. Bakery men and butchers and others were darting about everywhere in small carts pulled by dogs. Dogs are very useful animals here, and have to earn their keep. We were told that prior to our arrival it had been raining constantly, but now the weather is beautiful, except that it is too hot. Today, tomorrow and Wednesday we will be sightseeing, and at 7:30 AM Thursday we will take the train to Hamburg. You will receive my next letter from there, with a description of my Berlin adventures.

Paul [sic]

Hamburg   8/20 July 1860

In my last letter, chère et bonne Maman, I described my arrival in Berlin and promised to write from Hamburg about how I had spent my time in Berlin, and now I am fulfilling that promise.

After I took the letter to the post office, I went about on foot to familiarize myself a bit with the city. I went strolling along various streets, looked at interesting statues in the squares, and went back to the hotel three hours later, and not once did I have to ask directions to the Hôtel de Rome. In general I was very favorably impressed with Berlin, in spite of the all-pervasive military element. Actually, I am only annoyed that although we have borrowed uniforms from the Germans, as well as the sentry system, sentry houses, and even the stone mile markers along the road, we have not appropriated anything really useful, although we could well have done so.

Order and a systematic approach are obvious in every little detail, as well as thoughtfulness and practicality. For example, let's consider something very basic: carriage drivers. There are a good many of them here. They drive small four-passenger carriages drawn by a single horse. In each carriage a sign is posted indicating the cost in very simple terms: what the fee is for one, two, three or four persons, and how much per hour; every driver carries a watch in his pocket. The drivers are permitted to park in designated squares or streets, in a single row. The one who arrives first takes his place at the head of the line, and the others line up behind him in order. If you wish to go out, you give a signal, and the first driver in line takes you. No one is permitted to move out of his place in line. Because of this, unlike the situation in our country, there is no shouting here, no running about, no pushing, no offers of service and arguments abut pay, and no driver can say that he is busy or that his horse is tired. In such a case he would have to go to the end of the line. When you go out by the hour you show your watch to the driver, and he looks at his, and then you can ride to your heart's content. In short, there is the greatest sense of order in everything.

When I went back to the hotel after my stroll, I dined at the common table. There are common tables almost everywhere, where one pays 60 kopecks silver for dinner, not including wine. Dinner consists of six or seven courses and coffee; the food is well prepared and delicious everywhere. The ladies also appear at

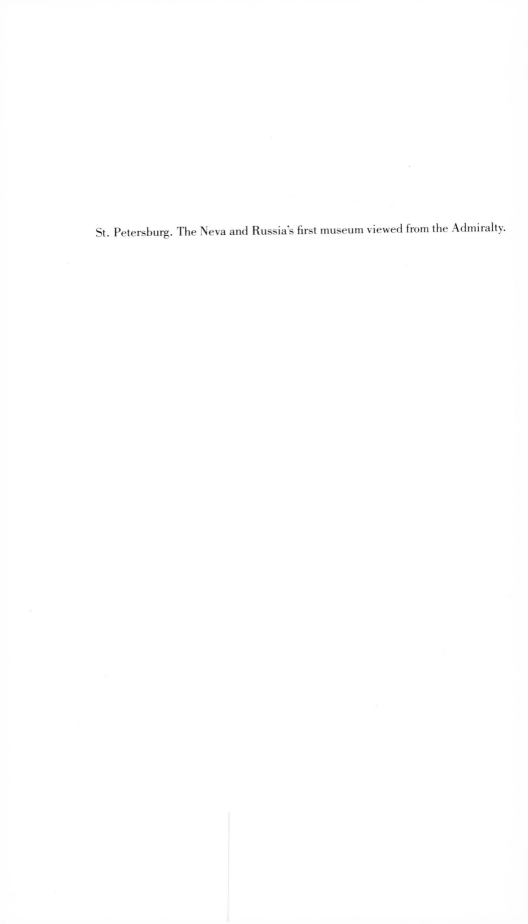

St. Petersburg. The Neva and Russia's first museum viewed from the Admiralty.

dinner. It is customary here for ladies to go everywhere alone. They go to the confectioner's shop to drink seltzer water or beer, or to eat ice cream.

After dinner Kostlivtsov and I went to a hotel where our shipboard acquaintances were staying, and then we went together with them to Charlottenburg, a small village like our Tsarskoe Selo, with a royal palace and many mementoes of Frederick the Great. There were several fine paintings and a superb marble statue of the Empress Alexandra Fedorovna, done during her youth. After we had seen the palace and the park we returned to Berlin, and since we still had some time, we went to see a little local outdoor fête. From there we went back to the hotel for supper.

The next day we again went out together and took the train to Potsdam, the favorite residence of the late monarch. The present monarch lives there also, in complete solitude. In Potsdam we bowed to the remains of Frederick the Great, saw the palace, the park, the orangerie, and Sans Souci, a famous millhouse, which the owner would not yield to the king, and which has ever since been preserved as a memorial. I will not describe all the details, for that would take too much time and space.

On Wednesday we went to see a new museum, spending the whole morning there, but even so we could only see it superficially. It is really amazing how Prussia, with its limited resources, manages to do so much so well. Not only has it not gone into debt, but there is still money left in the budget. The new museum is still not completely ready, but nonetheless from 12:00 until 4:00 everyone is allowed to enter, and they do not need permits or tickets. Soldiers, workmen, chambermaids, cooks—everyone goes there free of charge. They leave their walking sticks and umbrellas with the cloakroom attendant, and walk about freely. Occasionally there is a small charge for entry, but only on certain days. On all other occasions everyone may enter free of charge. All of these museums, galleries, et cetera are built with public money, and therefore justice demands that everyone be admitted without charge.

There are a good many Russians here, including Mt., who joined me at the hotel. We had dinner together twice at the common table. Since I had to meet with the agent of the [Russian] American Company, I left Berlin yesterday at 11:00, and today by 5:00 AM I was in Hamburg. Ols. came with me; he has been sightseeing with us in Berlin. Tomorrow Kostlivtsov will go to Dresden, and Ols. and I will join him there. We changed our itinerary slightly because we wanted to see Dresden. From there we will go to Frankfurt, Baden-Baden and Paris; from Paris we will go to Brussels and Ostend, and from there directly to London. Ols. will accompany us to Paris. He is a very fine gentleman, agreeable and inquisitive, and it is pleasant to be with him.

After we arrived in Hamburg today I took quarters in the Hôtel-Streit in the best part of town. Because there is a shortage of rooms in almost all the hotels, I had to take quarters on the fourth floor, but my windows open onto the street, and the view is splendid, with the city spread out before my eyes. I am paying about 60 kopecks per day for my rooms. Ols. is next to me. From the time I left Peterburg up to today I have spent nine gold pieces in all, which is about five rubles per day, including railroad trips, et cetera. And I am still in the early stage of my journey, when one is not very experienced in making arrangements. Later, when one is more familiar with local customs, one becomes more canny. Since I intend to stay only one day in Hamburg, I will hurry to finish this letter in order to spend time with the [Russian American Company] agent, and to wander about the city. And so—until the next letter.

Dresden   12/24 July 1860

The last letter I sent you was from Hamburg, chère et bonne Maman. You can see I am not lazy about writing, but indeed sit down to write a letter whenever I have a few free minutes. And so now, after spending the whole morning sightseeing in Dresden, I have had luncheon, and instead of taking a nap, I am writing this letter to you. At 5:00 Ols. and I will go out to see the city again until dusk; then we will go to a concert, and drink seltzer water under the shade of the nut trees. I wrote to you about my stay in Hamburg. When I had finished the letter, I set out to meet with the agent of the American Company, Vogel, but I could not find where he lived and so went back to the hotel and sent a messenger to him. I walked around the city until it was time to eat. I walked three hours, went along quite a few streets, and got a good feeling for the way the city is laid out. I had some oysters in a wine bar, and at 4:00 returned to the hotel to dine at the *table d'hôte*. I had dinner with Ols. and with another gentleman by the name of Bergholz, who had been traveling with us from Peterburg. The dinner was very good, with seven or eight courses plus dessert, and it cost 60 kopecks. This is the usual price in all the best hotels in Germany. After dinner Mr. Vogel appeared, and invited me to see the city. Of course I introduced him to Ols. and to Bergholz. We took a carriage and drove out to see the environs of the city, which are splendid. The city itself is also marvelously beautiful. We drove all evening. At 4:00 PM there were horse races outside the city, and we went to see them. The whole city was there, in stylish carriages. The horses had silver trappings and colorful ribbon rosettes. Vogel got splendid seats for us in a covered gallery, and we saw horse races which couldn't possibly have been better . . .

Dresden is one of the most beautiful cities in Germany. No wonder there are always throngs of Russians there, some of whom have lived in Dresden for a number of years. An elderly Russian lady who sat across from me at dinner said that she has taken a first-floor apartment here consisting of five rooms, furnished, including bed and table linens, china, silver, porcelain and crystal; for all of this she pays 200 thalers per year, which is about 180 silver rubles. It is understandable that such reasonable prices attract many persons. Good theater, freedom in one's way of life and the beautiful location all make life in Dresden especially delightful.

After we had seen the city and had had dinner at the common table, we set out to hear a concert on a terrace above the Elbe River. What a marvelous place! Crowds of people. Gentlemen come from work, sit at a little table, order a glass of lemonade or beer, and stay from 6:00 until 11:00 PM, paying an entrance fee of 15 silver kopecks. We also sat at a table, ordered a bottle of good Rhine wine, smoked cigars, and reveled in the superb evening.

I am not describing in detail all the sights I have had an opportunity to see, because that would take so much time. I am content to note everything briefly in my diary, so that subsequently all of this, if I am not too lazy and can find the time, will become a running account of my journey. Incidentally, do save my letters. They may help me verify dates and certain facts, in case I should decide to write a description of my trip. Really, a trip is a most enjoyable thing. It is only too bad to have to hurry. In Russia one can sometimes travel for a whole year without saying a word to anyone, but here, both on the train and at the common table, everyone strikes up conversations, and even young ladies are not at all surprised if a strange gentleman engages in conversation with them. They readily answer questions, and often, if they hear you ask someone a question he can't answer, they may join in the conversation and answer the question themselves. They do this simply and naturally, as a completely normal thing. I am a foreigner, they are natives, they know better than I the local customs, and willingly share their knowledge with me.

13/25 July 1860

After dinner yesterday I traveled through the countryside, which is extraordinarily picturesque. Today I saw an art gallery and other things, and this evening we will probably go out of the city to a concert and a fireworks display. Before I left Peterburg, Dr. Kr. advised me to eat as many grapes as possible. The grapes here are not ripe yet, so instead I drink their juice in the form of a superb Rhine wine, and eat vast quantities of cherries, which are

CIVIL AND SAVAGE ENCOUNTERS

almost free here, and are huge and delectable. If Kostlivtsov returns from Teplice today, then probably in the morning of the day after tomorrow we will contine on our way to Frankfurt, and from there go on the Rhine to Cologne in order to see the most picturesque sights along the river. You will probably receive the next letter from Frankfurt.

Only a few days have gone by since I left Peterburg, but how much I have traveled already, and how much I have seen!

Brussels   21 July/2 August 1860

On the 15th at 6:30 AM we took the express train from Dresden to Leipzig, and then we changed trains and went rapidly to Frankfurt am Main, where we arrived safely at 10:30 PM. We stayed in the Hôtel de l'Empereur Romain. You can see, chère et bonne Maman, how quickly a journey is accomplished here. A distance of more than 70 German miles, which is about 490 versts, took only 16 hours of travel in a pleasant railroad car. The next day we went out to see the city, and ordered a carriage to be ready to take us to drink the waters at Homburg. I like Frankfurt. The streets are quite wide and well maintained, the homes are large and well built, there are many fine shops, and there is a complete absence of police. Yet at the same time everyone on the streets is well behaved and quiet. One does not hear quarrels and shouting. Throughout Germany not even coachmen shout "*Padi*! ["make way"]" They just crack their whips, and each one steps aside to allow carriages to pass. Throughout my entire trip abroad, even on holidays, I have not seen a single drunk. At parties people have a good time and drink beer or wine, but they do not become drunk, which is unfortunately always the case in our country. People are generally polite and helpful, and quite willing to explain anything you may need to know. If you are on the street, for example, and stop someone to ask directions to some famous place, he will not only explain how to go there, but often will go out of his way to take you there. Generally speaking, in their own country the Germans are very admirable people, but it is too bad that they like to play at being little soldiers to such an extreme, and are so demented about form. Everyone here wants to wear some sort of formal decoration, from the generals right down to the streetsweepers.

After we had gone about the city, at 11:00 AM we took a fine carriage and drove along a beautiful road, with lovely fruit trees along both sides, which took us to Homburg. In recent years this little town has become a favorite place for people who come to take the cure. The mineral waters are said to cure all ills, but many are also attracted by roulette, and by the balls and concerts. We drove directly to the kur-saal or pumproom, where people stroll about from morning until night. There were already crowds of people there. I reserved places for us at the table d'hôte for 1:00 PM, and then we went to look about. The concert hall, dining room and the gaming rooms are all very fine. The garden proper is not large, but it is shady and well cared for. There is a superb promenade nearby, and the grounds are beautiful. When we entered the casino a great many persons were already milling about the gambling tables. At one group of tables they were playing roulette, and at other tables, *trente et quarante*. The silence was broken only by the voice of the croupier quietly announcing, "Faites le jeu, messieurs, le jeu est fait; rouge gagne; couleur perd," and by the sound of gold and silver coins being passed from the croupier to the winners and back again. We watched the games for a long time, but did not understand it all.

In the newspaper reading room there are many Russian periodicals, including *Peterburgskaia Vedomost, Severnaia Pchela* and *Invalid*. It was pleasant to glance through Russian papers; however you hear Russian spoken here every time you turn around, especially around the gambling tables, where our compatriots, both male and female, swarm like flies to honey. We stayed in Homburg until 6:00 PM, and then returned to Frankfurt and went out on foot to see if there were any musical performances. This is how we happened to go to the Zoological Garden where a

CIVIL AND SAVAGE ENCOUNTERS

military band was giving a concert. We sat at a little table until 11:00 and then strolled back to the hotel.

The next morning at 9:30 we took the train to Wiesbaden, via Mainz. Unfortunately the weather was abominable, with the rain coming down by the pailful. At 11:30 AM we reached Wiesbaden and took rooms in the Hotel Victoria. But then a new misfortune befell us: there were so many travellers there that we were given a little mousetrap of a room up under the roof with a dormer window. Everything is very clean, but in order to see what is happening on the street, I have to stand on a chair and poke my head out through the dormer, and I have to go up 80 steps to get to the room. However, there was nothing else to do, because we couldn't go out in the downpour to look for other quarters.

We had dinner in the hotel and then went to take the waters in the pumproom. The building is huge, and the rooms are beautiful. There is a spacious garden, an enormous concourse, hordes of Russians, and the gambling is even livelier than in Homburg. We spent the evening there, had supper, and returned to the hotel.

The next day the weather was somewhat better, so we took a carrage and went out to see the Orthodox church where Elisaveta Mikhailovna is entombed, which was built by her husband. We purposely went early, hoping to be there in time for a mass, but unfortunately mass is only sung on holidays. The church is located outside the city on a hill which for some reason is called Neronova. The view from there is charming. Wiesbaden and its environs are in the palm of one's hand. It would have been quite impossible to have chosen a better location, surrounded as it is by endless orchards of fruit trees where pears, apples, walnuts, cherries and the like are all mingled. The exterior of the church is very lovely, with gilded cupolas, and the interior is all done in marble. The iconostasis is the work of Neff. On the left there is a little chapel with the tomb of Elisaveta Mikhailovna. Her sepulchre is of white marble, and on top is a lifesize statue of her in a reclining position, a superb piece. The choir is Bohemian, and the members are said to sing very well although they do not understand a word of Russian.

Returning to the city, we left the carriage and walked about seeing Wiesbaden. We made our appearance in the pumproom at dinner time. We spent the rest of the day there listening to lovely music, reading, strolling through the gardens, and watching all the people. I took a turn at the table and put one gold piece on rouge. At first I won 50 rubles, but then I gambled it away and stopped playing, deciding it was safer to keep the money in my pocket than to risk it on the green baize field.

On the 19th at 10:00 AM we hired a carriage, had our bags put on it, and went to the little town of Biberach on the Rhine, where we were to take a steamer to go down the Rhine to Cologne. We reached Biberach at 11:00, and since we had an hour and a half until we sailed, we decided to have a little stroll through the town. But it happened that an acquaintance of Kostlivtsov's lived right near the harbor, and had just arrived in Biberach the day before. When he saw us from his balcony, he immediately sent his man after us and gave us breakfast, so we went directly from his house to the ship. There were so many passengers that at first we couldn't find a place to sit, but soon everything got straightened out, especially when they set up places for the table d'hôte on both sides of the deck. Of course we sat at a table with other persons, and while dining we feasted our eyes on the picturesque shores of the Rhine. The best places are between Mainz, a little above Biberach, and Koblenz. Beyond Koblenz the shore is quite flat, and there is nothing of great interest all the way to Cologne. However, listening to the tales of the travelers, I might have supposed I was seeing something exceptional all along the Rhine, and probably I might have thought so too, if I had not seen the Caucasus last fall. But here on the Rhine the interest is in all the ruined castles, almost every one of which has its own legends. All these scattered little towns are surrounded by vineyards and cultivated fields. Everywhere one sees the results of peaceful industrious work, and every plot of ground has been cultivated. Historical reminiscences are associated with all these places which glide past your eyes like a shimmering panorama. It requires a good deal of effort from one's imagination and memory to recall the past, from feudal times to the present.

In spite of a brisk headwind, the ship carried us rapidly along with the current, and by 7:30 we reached Cologne. We were taken directly to the Hôtel de Bellevue on the right bank of the Rhine. After we had tea and unpacked, we walked into the city, roaming along various streets, and finally returned to the hotel and went to bed. At 9:00 the next morning we again set out on foot to visit the famous Cologne cathedral, which is presently being restored so that part of it is to be left as it was in the old days, but the other part is being rebuilt in the same style. In order to have a clear understanding of how the cathedral will look after the restoration is complete, we went into a shop where they sell Maria Farion's own Eau de Cologne; there is a model of the cathedral there, reduced to 1/60 actual size. It is built of wood, iron and papier maché. The artist spent several years working on it, and it is quite remarkable. In general the architecture of the cathedral is superb, and the workmanship is beautiful, almost like lace.

After we had seen the cathedral, we went to the Church of St. Ursula, built on the very spot where St. Ursula had been killed together with 11,000 Christian maidens. The church itself is not especially noteworthy, but there is one chapel where they have preserved the skulls of St. Ursula and the maidens who were killed with her, and all the walls are decorated from top to bottom with their bones. The skulls, each with a velvet fillet on which the name of the martyr is written in gold and precious stones, are kept in a cabinet with glass windows. In the middle of the chapel under a glass bell, St. Ursula's right leg has been preserved, along with a piece of arrowhead found in her heart, the remnants of her garments, and the skull of her betrothed. In a glass box are two needles from the Savior's crown of thorns, and a stone (actually a marble) amphora, one of those in which the Savior transformed water into wine.

After we had paid homage to Ursula's remains, we returned to the hotel and at 1:30 went by train through Aachen to Brussels. The road to Verviers passes through such gorgeous places that it appeals to me more than the banks of the Rhine. It is true that the land here is not so cultivated, but on the other hand there are factories and industrial buildings everywhere, all spread out in such beautiful areas. You observe, and you are lost in admiration. Between Cologne and Brussels we went through 22 tunnels and crossed several bridges and viaducts. The train flies like a bird along level, beautifully laid rails. Our train had 15 cars and only two conductors, but this was quite enough to keep everything in order, in spite of the fact that at every station new passengers boarded and others got off, and at some stations two or three trains met. Everyone seems to know what he may do, and what he should not do, and therefore there is no need for prisons or for police. In Verviers, Belgian customs officials inspected our baggage, but they were just as considerate as the Prussian officials had been and did not disturb anything, and took our word that we did not have any contraband.

A few stations beyond Verviers there is a hill which is so steep the train can only ascend it with the assistance of a steel cable, which is operated by means of a machine; but even this operation is accomplished very readily. We were only detained by the fact of having too many cars, so the train had to go up the hill in two sections. In Verviers I talked with the conductor, treating him in a kindly and polite manner as an equal. I gave him a cigar, and he reciprocated by giving Kostlivtsov and me an eight-passenger compartment all to ourselves all the way to Brussels. He managed to put all the passengers in other compartments, and left us alone so that we could lie down, sit, and do as we pleased. I must comment on the fact that in Germany smoking is usually permitted in all the cars; but whereas in Russia special cars are set aside for those who wish to smoke, here first and second class cars have special compartments for *non-smokers*. Thus it was very convenient for us to be able to smoke, as it would have been difficult to travel for 16 hours without smoking. The train does stop frequently, but it is only for one or two or three minutes at most, and then it starts up again. Anyone who wishes to have something to eat takes bread and butter or something of that nature with him, or waits until one of the rare times when the train is in the station

CIVIL AND SAVAGE ENCOUNTERS

for 10 or 15 minutes to change cars or the like. However, at each station little boys come to the train from cafes, bringing bread and butter, beer, wine and fruit, and you can always buy whatever you need.

We reached Brussels at 10:00 PM. Today we arose at 6:30 as usual, and at 9:00 we went to see the national column which was erected by the people to honor the present monarch [King Leopold I] who is deservedly much beloved here. We also saw the National Assembly and the Senate. Along the walls there are allegorical statues with inscriptions such as "Les belges sont libres" and "Liberté de la presse." Later we drove to the cathedral, which is being rebuilt in the same manner as the Cologne cathedral. It has particularly beautiful stained glass windows, and a carved wooden pulpit which is especially interesting. In the front, life-sized Adam and Eve are being expelled from paradise by the angel, and Death is following them. The tail of the serpent is between them; the serpent itself is entwined about the entire pulpit between trees, and it is raising its head above the top of the pulpit; but the head is being stamped down by the foot of the Savior, who is supported by the Mother of God holding a cross in her arms. At the base of the pulpit, between the trees, the seven deadly sins are depicted as animals: the peacock (pride); a monkey eating fruit (gluttony); a rooster (lust); an eagle (anger); a fox (envy); a parrot (sloth); and one other I don't remember. The workmanship is astonishing.

From the cathedral we went to look at the memorial built by the people to commemorate those who lost their lives during the [1831] revolution. Eight hundred persons are buried at the base of the memorial, and their names are inscribed on plaques. The bas-reliefs on the memorial show the most important events of the revolution, and there are likenesses of the principles. They have portrayed the uprising, the hope, the struggle and the victory! Honor and Glory to those who know how to respect the memory of the men who shed blood for them. On a special plaque there is the decree which authorizes the construction of this memorial, and which takes the widows and orphans of those who were killed under the protection of the fatherland! . . .

Then we went to see the lace factory, where 2,000 young girls and women are employed to make lace. No wonder some kinds of lace are so expensive, when each piece is handmade by an expert needlewoman, and a single piece may require as much as 40 days of constant work. After the lace factory we visited the local Rathaus and returned home in time for dinner. Now we are getting together to listen to music in the Zoological Garden, and tomorrow we are planning to go to the battlefield of Waterloo; then on to Paris.

Paul

Paris   28 July/9 August 1860

Chère et bonne Maman, the last letter I wrote you was from Brussels, and I ended it by saying that the next day we were planning to go the battlefield of Waterloo. This plan failed to materialize, however, because it rained from morning on, and we were not interested in traveling some 14 versts in such weather. And so at about 10:00 in the morning I went to the Catholic cathedral to pray for you, chère Maman, and then we went sightseeing, which we had not had a chance to do the previous day. Fortunately the weather cleared after midday, but it was then too late to go to Waterloo, and so we continued to stroll about the city. To tell the truth, there are very few sights to see in Brussels, and all the curiosities can be seen in a few hours. In the evening we went to a concert in a park on the same square where our hotel is located. The concert reminded me very much of our Bezborodko* and former royal concerts, because of their monotony. It is true that the music is very fine, but the audience wanders around, just as at home, and they carry on whispered conversations, and at 10:00 everything closes up and everyone rushes home to go to bed.

---

*Aleksandr Andreevich Bezborodko (1747-99), Secretary to Catherine II.—Eds.

On the morning of 23 July at 8:30 we took the train to Paris. There were only five of us in our car, and our companions turned out to be very pleasant, one in particular who is a naval officer and commands a frigate. We chatted the whole way, asked them about Parisian life, and their advice was most helpful. In this manner time passed imperceptibly, and at 5:30 in the evening we came into Paris at full speed from the direction of Montmartre. We were delayed for about half an hour at the station while customs officials inspected our baggage, but actually we had very little with us, having sent our large trunks directly to Paris from Dresden, and so it all went along with no problems. We put our bags and small valises on an omnibus, and then we got inside and in ten minutes we were on the Avenue de St. Honoré at the Hôtel de France et de Bath. We were given very good quarters consisting of two bedrooms, a sitting room and a dining room; we pay 12 francs per day, without meals. The hotel is very well kept up. It was recommended to us by Mns., Kostlivtsov's uncle, whose father is married to Ob., the owner of the hotel. She is a very lovely lady and welcomed us most warmly and is constantly concerned about our comfort. Kostlivtsov was tired from the journey and stayed in the hotel, but as usual I set out on foot to see Paris by its evening lights. I walked through the Place Vendôme and came out on the Boulevard des Italiens. What a sense of life everywhere! Throngs of people, cafes all lighted and shops as well, and how amazingly fine they are! Strolling along the boulevard I came to the Café Anglais, one of the best in Paris, had supper there, and returned to the hotel, still on foot.

The 24th was Sunday. At 10:00 AM we went the Russian church. There were many people, and the service was excellent. Among other persons I recognized Btk., Mt., Shvl. and others. After church we went to the Nôtre Dame de Paris, and from there to the Palais Royale. Here our finances received their first jolt: there are so many stores that one's eyes go wild wanting to buy things. Fortunately we are somewhat restrained by the fact that the [return] route across Siberia* will make it difficult to carry much with us.

---

*Golovin and Kostlivtsov had orders to return from Alaska to St. Petersburg via Siberia; this plan was changed. —Eds.

On the evening of the 24th we went to the Gymnase Dramatique theater. They were performing *Les Deux Timides*, a farce which was very well presented, and *Les Faux Bons Hommes*, which we had seen in Peterburg and which is causing a great furor here. On the morning of the 25th we saw Les Invalides and the tomb of Napoleon I, and in the evening went to the Opéra Comique where there was a very satisfactory performance of the operetta *Le Domino Noir*. There are no Italian operas being performed now, since the season has ended, but we will be hearing opera in London. On the 26th we went to Ste. Chapelle, built by St. Louis, which was ravaged during the first revolution and is now being restored to its former appearance. We also went to the Musée de Cluny, where there is a fine collection of antiques, to the Luxembourg Gallery, the Panthéon with its monument to Voltaire and Jean-Jacques Rousseau, and finally the Jardin des Plantes with its superb zoo. Here I saw a rather strange thing: a crane with a wooden leg. This crane had broken its leg, and the leg would not heal, so they amputated it below the knee and attached a wooden leg made of sugar cane. The crane can run about quite remarkably. There are all kinds of animals here, from pigs to lions, elephants to hippopotamuses, chickens to eagles, frogs to crocodiles, and silkworms to a boa constrictor. The zoological garden is beautifully arranged, with every kind of vegetation, and there are always crowds of people because there is no admission charge.

I also saw something unique: a piece of Molière's lower jaw. A sign says that during the first revolution the national convention conceived the idea of ordering the bones of great men of France to be exhumed, and ordered a special committee of scholars to try to make clay from the bones, and then to make cups from the clay, and lastly to inscribe on the cups the names of the persons from whose bones the cups had been made. The bones were exhumed and taken to a special building where experiments were to be conducted. The proposal was never carried out, however, and so the bones were reburied; but one of the scholars secretly carried off a piece of Molière's jaw and now has presented it to the Musée de Cluny. Can you imagine such a wild notion! There is also a very richly embroidered cope here which belonged to the Archbishop of Paris. It was probably made in the East, because on the back of the vestment there are Turkish letters which say, "There is no God but God and Mohammed is His Prophet." The Archbishop wore this cope, and since he had no knowledge of Turkish characters, he did not realize what the inscription said.

That evening we went to the Champs Elysées, and to the Empress Circus. The circus is magnificent. Edwards, an old acquaintance from Peterburg, shows his trained dogs, and there is a remarkably fine gymnast named Léotard. He preforms such feats in the air that one's hair stands on end. Yesterday we spent the whole morning at the Louvre. We went there at 10:30 and left at 4:00 in the afternoon when the gallery closed. There were many people there because admission is free. In the Chambre des Souverains they have brought together all manner of things that belonged to the kings of France. Most of the items belonged to Napoleon I and to his son. They have uniforms and parade dress on display as museum pieces.

After dinner we went to the Chateau des Fleurs, which is something like the Bal Mabille but a bit more modest. Nevertheless the cancan is going strong there too, and while we were there, two gentlemen were escorted out who were dancing rather scandalously. The Chateau des Fleurs is very well built with a stage for the musicians, and everything lighted with gas lights and with colorful lanterns. In front of the stage there is a large area where the sand has been tamped down and rolled. In the middle there are enormous candelabra with gas lights, and all around are colored lamps and little globes, paths for those who wish to promenade, and little pavilions for persons who wish to drink wine. The sanded area is also used as a dance floor. There are very few nice girls. For the most part there are women of faded beauty who are heavily powdered and made up. They say that in the Mabille there are many more nice women—we shall see, because we are going there Saturday, the day everyone goes.

I did not finish my letter because I went out to look at the city, but now I am continuing it. On the 28th we went out rather late just to look at some of the back streets of Paris. It is certainly frustrating to see how well built everything is here, and then to think how backward we are in everything. Everywhere there are beautiful streets and smooth stone roadways. It is clean everywhere, and neat. Butcher shops and fruit stands are so beautifully arranged that it is a pleasure to look at them. Beef is displayed either on wooden tables covered with linen of irreproachable whiteness, or on marble stands. Butchers wear clean white coats and aprons, never stained the way our butchers' are. In short, you go into a butcher shop as if you were going into any fine shop. Even the narrowest lane in the remotest part of the city is lighted with gas. There is running water everywhere. Coaches run in all directions, and passengers can transfer from one to another. One can go all the way from one end of Paris to the other for just a few sous, and the coaches are neatly and properly kept up. The pair of horses harnessed to a coach is chosen from a sturdy breed, always well fleshed. They are full of vigor and run quickly, not the way our jaded nags do, when they have a hard time just barely moving down Nevskii Prospekt*, even though these coaches are larger and passengers sit both inside and on top. As for the fiacres, I cannot say that they are all so good. Some are quite dandy, harnessed to a very good horse, but there are also some that have a rather worn-out horse pulling with some difficulty.

I dined alone because Kostlivtsov had gone to see Mns. outside the city. After dinner I went to the Théatre de Palais Royale where a new play was being given, *Mémoires de Mimi Bamboche*. It is a farce in which gentlemen from the Mabille are found out, altogether in the French manner, and the public loves it, especially since it is so well done. Yesterday I went to the Champs de Mars, where large parades are held. This square is at least six times the size of our Tsaritsyn

---

*The main avenue of St. Petersburg and of present Leningrad.—Eds.

CIVIL AND SAVAGE ENCOUNTERS

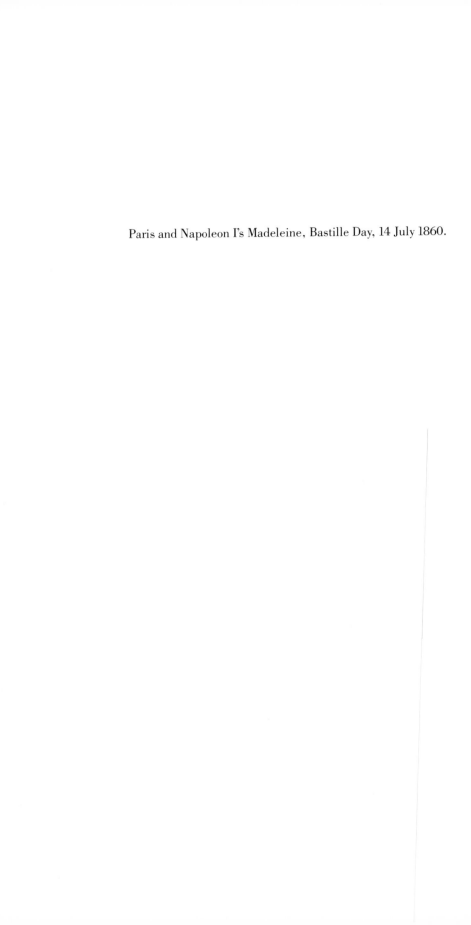

Paris and Napoleon I's Madeleine, Bastille Day, 14 July 1860.

Field. Then I went back to the Champs Elysées, and in the evening Kostlivtsov and I went to the Bois de Boulogne to the Chalet. We wanted to see the Pré Catalan, but unfortunately this building which is famous for its elegant lighting is closed at the present. Today we had planned to see the Gobelin factory in the morning and go to the Mabille in the evening, but I don't know whether the latter will be possible, since it is raining now and looks as if it may keep on all day.

Our intention had been to leave here on Tuesday, and be in London Wednesday, Thursday and Friday, then leave on Saturday for New York; but there is a great holiday here on Wednesday. The whole city of Paris will be illuminated, and there will be a huge parade in the Champs de Mars, and so we have decided to stay here for another week and leave for London on Saturday. Then seven days later, August 13 by our calendar, we will leave for New York. You can't go to Rome without seeing the Pope, and you can't leave Paris without seeing Napoleon [III] . . .

Paris   3/15 August 1860

We took advantage of a brief letup in the rain to go off to see the Gobelin factory where they weave tapestries and the like. What a marvelous place! What workmanship! What colors! These are not textiles, but paintings. One immediately realizes that these are genuinely paintings of famous artists, not just copies woven in wool. Portraits of Louis Napoleon and the Empress really seem to come alive. We regarded the entire manufacturing process at great length. No wonder these items are so expensive. It takes not only a fine craftsman to create these, but an artist as well, and of course everything has to be done very slowly by hand. I walked through the rooms for a long time because I wanted to see everything and to watch them work. Afterward we went to see a marvelous building they call Les Halles, which is actually a haymarket where one can buy poultry, meat, vegetables, etc. After that we went back to the hotel. Les Halles is entirely built of iron and glass. There is a massive cover over the entire square, with stalls set up under it to sell produce. The name of each merchant is posted on a board that hangs over his or her stall. Everything is so neat it is a delight to look at. Any further excursions were interrupted by rain which came down in buckets until night.

On Sunday we went to our church; I met Ols. there, who had just arrived in Paris yesterday, and since he did not know where we were staying, he looked for us in church. In the evening we went to the Théatre des Varietés, where a rather silly fantasy was being presented, *La Fille du Diable*; but it is quite successful here because it is well presented and is filled with puns and sharp-edged wit, which the French are quite partial to. On Monday we went to the office of the English South East Steamship Company to buy tickets for the voyage from Liverpool to Boston, and we were just barely able to get tickets because so many emigrants are going to America. We paid 550 francs for our accommodations, about 137.50 silver rubles. We arranged for our large steamer trunks to be sent directly to Liverpool, while we will go to London and stay until Friday the 24th, which is the 12th by our calendar, and on the 13th we will leave from Liverpool for Boston and go from there by train to New York. This will give us the opportunity to gain two days and save 75 francs.

Yesterday still another of our Berlin acquaintances, Prts., came to Paris and stayed with us; in the evening he and Kostlivtsov and I went to the Bal Mabille. It is such a beautiful little garden, and is so wonderfully and tastefully lighted by gas. It was a pleasure to stay there until twelve when the ball ended.

4/16 August 1860

I am writing to you while I still have vivid impressions of yesterday's festivities. I will start by saying that a few days ago the *Monitor* published the program for the national holiday on the 15th in honor of the Emperor, as always is the case; immediately afterward an endless horde of placard peddlers and magazine vendors appeared on all the streets with copies of the program. "Voici le programme de la fête national de 15, fête de Sa Majesté l'Empereur Napoleon II, un sou, messieurs et mesdames! Grande fête!! Illuminations!! Régattes!! Un sou!!" The cry resounded all through Paris. Of course we bought one of these programs and made arrangements to hire an open carriage on the morning of the 15th so we could watch all the preparations, and then in the evening we planned to drive all around to see the illuminations.

The four of us, Kostlivtsov, Prts., Ols. and I, decided to go together, but unfortunately poor Ols. developed a high fever so instead of celebrating he had to spend the whole day in bed. In the morning a very dandy carriage and a pair of horses came for us; we had hired it for the entire day for 30 francs, which is about 7.50 silver rubles. at first there was a light rain, but the skies cleared about 11:00 AM, and it warmed up so that people began to wander about in all the streets. The three of us first went to see the Hôtel de Ville all decorated with flags, and then we went to the Seine where there was a sloop race between the Alma and Invalides bridges. Then we went to the Esplanade des Invalides where two theaters had been built, and there were many booths with conjurors and rope dancers. Four tall columns with various prizes on top had been set up for those who wanted to test their skill. The same kinds of amusements had also been set up at the Place du Trône, and at 1:00 PM there were free peformances in all the theaters in the city.

In order to get a seat, people began lining up in front of the ticket offices at 6:00 AM, so that many ate breakfast right on the street without leaving their places in line; but there was no crush, because it is a generally accepted rule here to follow this procedure to get tickets: a wooden partition is set up in front of a ticket office, so that a double line can easily be formed between the partition and the wall. A police sergeant is stationed at the entry into this improvised corridor, and he watches to see that people enter in twos. Everyone is so accustomed to this that people who come along later simply line up in pairs forming the line, or as there say here, *Faire la queue*. If anyone comes along and tries to go to the head of the line, he is immediately taken off by the police, or else the people in line would give him his due. When they hand out theater tickets in the evening, you always see a line of people in front of the door waiting their turns to take tickets and enter the theater. These queues had formed in front of the theaters by 6:00 AM.

The whole city had a most festive appearance. All the homes were decorated with flags, banners and garlands. Illuminations were being prepared everywhere. Only here the illuminations are arranged more tastefully than in Petersburg: the garlands with tiny bulbs are not hung on the walls of the homes, but between the lanterns on the streets. Various decorations are placed above the lanters, either little globes, or the lantern itself may be removed and into the gas tube they insert a monogram, a star, and eagle, or perhaps a crown. In this manner a superb and unusually beautiful espalier is created out of the garlands and various decorations; it goes along both sides of the street, from one end to the other, and the homes remain free of soot.

But I must tell you everything in proper order. We watched the boat race, or as they call it, the regatta. Then we went to the Place des Invalides and on to the Esplanade. In order to give the people more space, vehicular travel through the Esplanade and adjacent streets was barred. Imagine a square wider and longer than our Admiralty, with trees on all sides. The whole square has theaters and booths lining its sides. Under the trees are many little stands where they sell wine, beer and other refreshments. There are so many people you can scarcely move through the crowd. Everyone chatters, moves about, laughs, jokes, but no one is drunk. Some, of course, are very jolly, but they behave themselves and do not loll about on the roadway. One sees scarcely any uniformed policemen, but there are plenty of them in the adjacent streets, and in amongst the people there are plainclothes policemen whom one doesn't notice. They are there only in case someone causes a real problem.

CIVIL AND SAVAGE ENCOUNTERS

We milled about among the people for quite some time. We were approached by various peddlers selling cakes, sugar candy and the like. They not only sell refreshments, but they also offer them as prizes for lotteries and other games. For example, several men will gather at a peddler's little table; each pays a kopeck, and the money is put on two long boards with numbers printed on them that look rather like the cards used in Lotto. Then the man throws a little ball into the number wheel, and the person on whose number the ball stops receives a large cake. If two numbers come up, one below the other, both belonging to the same person, that forms an ambo, and the winner receives a special prize of a honeycake. The ball is thrown as many times as there are players, and of course it often falls on empty numbers. The winners go on stuffing their stomachs with cakes, and the losers again stake a kopeck, or go to find some satisfaction in a free performance in one of the stalls.

When we had gone all around the Esplanade of the Place des Invalides, we took the carriage again and went to the Champs Elysées, and from there went back to the hotel for dinner. When we reached the hotel we dismissed the driver so he could go feed his horses, with the understanding that he was to return for us at 7:00 pm. By 8:00, however, our carriage had still not reappeared, and since by then there was no possibility of hiring any kind of vehicle at all, we decided to walk. As it happened, the driver's failure to reappear was definitely to our advantage. In the first place we saved 30 francs, and in the second, the carriage would not have been allowed into any of the illuminated streets anyway; these streets were reserved for pedestrians. I find this altogether reasonable, because it allows the people to go all through Paris to see everything without any shoving or elbowing.

We went directly into the Jardin de Tuileries, just a few steps from our hotel. The gardens were beautifully illuminated. The main allée leading from the court to the Place de la Concorde was lighted by gas, with garlands of various colored bulbs, and it was a most marvelous spectacle. The Place de la Concorde impressed us with its delightful lighting. Further on, the main allée of the Champs Elysées goes all the way to l'Etoile, where the Arc de

Triomphe is located. The whole way from the Tuileries to the Arc de Triomphe was lighted in the most diverse and wonderful manner; it looked like a fiery corridor about five versts in length, edged with great trees—and in the middle there was the Place de la Concorde, ablaze with thousands of colored flames, with all the statues and fountains. What a gorgeous miracle! We feasted our eyes on this charming sight and then went to the Seine, and from the bank we watched the spectacular fireworks display from the Champs de Mars. A bouquet created from thousands of colorful rockets with parachutes was devastatingly beautiful.

We kept walking and went along to the Hôtel de Ville. As we approached we stopped, thunderstruck by the splendor of the spectacle. Imagine an immense building in ancient gothic architecture, decorated with flags, golden eagles and various armatures, from top to bottom, done with exceptional taste, and with millions of gas flames on all the cornices. There were so many that this famous building, formerly a witness to so much revolution, looked like a magic castle from some fairy tale. The huge square in front of the building was so lighted up that one could imagine himself in an immense ballroom. The square was crowded with thousands of people all laughing and joking, but there was no shouting or rude language, and no danger of being stepped on by horses, because as I mentioned, coaches were not permitted in that whole length that we walked. From the Hôtel de Ville we walked along the street and finally came out on the Boulevard des Italiens. There were throngs of people everywhere, and laughter, conversation, yet everywhere there was order.

We went back to the hotel at midnight, so tired we could scarcely walk another step, but delighted with all we had seen, and with the greatest sensation of pleasure. But I must add that there is also a certain amount of bittersweet pain, when I compare the situation here with ours at home. Here you look, you love it all, and at the same time envy and disappointment make your heart heavy. Are we really less intelligent than all these people? Couldn't we have something like this? Or even better? Why are we so backward? Why is it so difficult for us to progress? I pray God that our children will not have to make such sad comparisons, especially hard for those who so ardently love their native land.

6/18 August 1860

It has been raining all day long, but at least there are now and then a few moments of good weather when one can stroll about and look at the city. Yesterday we took our large trunks to the steamship company office so they could be sent directly on to Liverpool. We are not leaving until Tuesday morning, because my portrait will not be ready until Monday. It would be so pleasant to live here and not have to do anything, but I must be off on my journey . . .

London   10/22 August 1860

In my last letter I wrote you that we had planned to leave Paris on Saturday, but that we later postponed our departure for two more days. The cause of this delay was the fact that certain items Kostlivtsov had bought were not going to be ready until Monday, and my portrait also. On Saturday, the 6th, we went with Ols. to see a performance in the hippodrome. It is an enormous building which can accommodate five or six thousand spectators. The circus arena is about a verst in circumference, and the spectacles are presented in the open air. Fortunately it did not rain, and we sat outside very comfortably. Three Polish performers were very good; they walked on two tightropes that had been stretched on an incline the whole length of the circus to a height of almost 100 feet. The two walked side by side, holding a pole in their hands, and a third person stood on the pole on one foot. In this manner they went all the way up to the very top, and then came back down again. The horses are also very fine. The performance began at 3:00 PM and ended at 5:30. From the hippodome we went to have dinner in a fine restaurant, the Philippe, and from there at 8:00 we went to the Opéra Comique to hear *Etoile du Nord*. The singers were French, and I cannot say that they were very good, but I enjoyed listening to Meyerbeer's music.

On the 7th after church Kostlivtsov, Ols., Prts. and I took the train to Versailles. All the fountains were playing that day, and crowds of people were wandering through the rooms of the court and in the gardens. Unfortunately it was raining all day so that we had to walk under umbrellas the whole time. After we had seen the gallery we went into the garden. At 5:00 they turned on the fountains; they are very beautiful, but in my opinion ours at Peterhof are better. The fountains were turned off at 6:30, and we went to have dinner; by 9:00 we were back in Paris, and since it was no longer raining, we sat at a cafe on the boulevard until midnight. I really love to sit out on the boulevard in the evening. The cafes and restaurants are lighted up with countless gas lights, all reflected in mirrors that decorated the buildings from top to bottom. There was a great crowd of people, all chattering, noisy, laughing. Truly, it is a joyous and lovely picture.

On Monday we went with Ols. to visit the cemetery of Père LaChaise, which is very large and nicely maintained, and the view of Paris from there is spectacular. We dined at Philippe's again, and that evening we went to the Théatre du Vaudeville to see a play called *Ce qui plaît aux femmes*. The play was rather boring, but there were some good moments. At 8:00 Tuesday morning Kostlivtsov and I boarded the train along with Prts., whom we had persuaded to accompany us to London. We reached Calais at 5:00 PM, and immediately were transferred to a small steamer. At 7:00 PM we reached Dover, again took a train, and at 10:00 PM we were in London. It is marvelous how fast these commuter trains run! The train is so swift that it fairly takes your breath away. The sea travel was pleasant, but Kostlivtsov was seasick.

In London we stayed at the Hotel Sablonière on Leicester Square. The hotel is not very good, but adequate since we only plan to stay here for two days. In Brighton we went to the railroad

CIVIL AND SAVAGE ENCOUNTERS

station to buy tickets to the Crystal Palace. What a spectacular building! How boldly it is conceived, and how masterfully executed! We went through the entire palace from top to bottom, looking at machines and agricultural equipment as well as at all the flowers, and every possible sort of industrial product. It is too bad that the rain never let up all day long, so that we were prevented from seeing the gardens properly. After we had had a good dinner in the Crystal Palace we returned to London, and went to look at the tunnel under the Thames. This structure is also bold and wonderful, but quite useless.

On the 11th/23rd we took a carriage and went out to see the sights of London. Of course we could only see things superficially; it would take at least a year to see things in serious detail. First of all we went to the Tower of London which was formerly a prison, and there we saw ancient weapons, suits of armor, instruments of torture, the block and the axe with which they beheaded people, the crown jewels, the dungeons, etc. From the Tower we went to the docks where commercial ships are loaded and unloaded. Over a distance of more than three miles they have built huge stone warehouses seven stories high. This whole area is so chock-full that for lack of space the yards are piled high with boxes, barrels and packets. What tremendous wealth there is here! This is industry that really *is* industry! . . .

Then we went to the Customs House, the Stock Exchange, City Hall, the banks, St. Paul's Cathedral, and finally, Westminster Abbey. It rained almost the whole time, but this didn't interfere with our sightseeing. Everything was very interesting, but London itself does not make a very pleasant impression. All the buildings and homes are covered with a layer of soot, so that everything is black and dirty. The statue of Wellington on his horse is as black as a chimneysweep. The streets are dirty, too. But the activity and all the movement are unique. It is impossible to take a step without encountering several omnibuses. However all of this hustle and bustle only goes on until evening; then all the activity slows down, most of the warehouses are closed, and the activity only continues in the taverns. Cafes such as one finds in Paris do not exist here.

Generally speaking, the English have a hard time being light-hearted. In a word, I have no desire to live in London. But in Paris—that's another matter. There one can live well and happily and inexpensively, not in a hotel, of course, but in a rented apartment or a furnished room. My acquaintance, Krl., rented an apartment in the best part of town on the rue de Rivoli; it is on the first floor, or the entresol as the French call it, so that one has to go up only about 15 steps on a beautiful staircase to reach it. There are six rooms, not large, but newly decorated, and there are mirrors over the fireplaces. He pays 35 silver rubles per month for this, or 420 silver rubles per year. In other sections of town one can find a similar apartment for even less money. Kostlivtsov and I had four rooms in a hotel and thus paid more than usual, but we had service, meals, did not stint on anything, took carriages and every day went to cafes and theaters—in short, we had every comfort and in spite of all this, my total costs for almost 20 days in Paris were about 200 silver rubles. I am fully convinced that for 2,000 rubles it would be possible to live abroad more than half a year very comfortably. Of course that would not include purchases . . .

12/24 August 1860

Today at 2:00 PM we are leaving for Liverpool, and tomorrow morning we will transfer to the steamer *Canada* and continue on our journey to Boston. The time for parties is coming to an end, and soon we will have to get down to work. It will be somewhat tedious on Sitka [Island], but I have had my share of new impressions for a long time, and God willing, I will be so busy working that I won't be aware of the month passing. You will receive my next letter from New York.

Paul

Aboard the steamer *America*,
Newfoundland in view   23 August/4 September 1860

This is the first day I have had a chance to do anything, chère et bonne Maman, and I am taking advantage of this situation to start my written conversation with you, although I may have to complete this letter after I reach Boston.

London did not make a very favorable impression on me because it rained every minute of our stay there. It is filthy everywhere. All the homes, all the statues are black with soot. But there is much of interest to see and to marvel at. Generally speaking people lead rather boring lives there, because of various prejudices which prevent true gentlemen from doing this and that. For example we almost had to force our guide to show us an inn where we could have breakfast. He kept making excuses, saying that gentlemen always have breakfast at home, and when he had to give in at last, he saw to it that our carriage stayed about 200 paces from the inn; he took us there and then left quickly, so no one would realize he was with us. This was both amusing and annoying. After we had seen everything we could in London, on the 24th we went to Liverpool, which we reached that same evening. The hotel there seemed like a palace compared to the one in London, and to our surprise, the prices were quite reasonable.

At noon on the 25th we boarded a small steamer which in ten minutes took us out to the *America* which was anchored in the middle of the river. It quickly loaded baggage, took on the post, and at 1:30 PM, raised anchor. I must tell you that *America* is one of the company's very worst ships. It has been in service for 12 years already, and is used only on special occasions. It was just our misfortune that the *Canada*, which we were supposed to have taken, is out of commission, and they have substituted *America*. Accommodations for the passengers are not too bad, thank heaven, but far from good, either. To boot, from the time we left Liverpool we have had strong winds, and since the ship constantly leaks in both her bow and stern, the deck is knee deep in water. It is impossible to move around in my cabin in the bow of the ship without having a cold sea water bath. This was particularly bad on the 27th and 28th when the wind blew like a fury, without a letup, for 48 hours; it approached hurricane proportions. Even now all my clothing, my boots and everything else are still soaking wet. The whole cabin is wet too, but in spite of all this, thank God I am in perfect health. For the entire five days Koslivtsov has been lying in his berth without being able to eat anything. He is just now beginning to become accustomed to the motion of the ship. It is strange that children, of whom there are six or seven aboard, are quite unaffected by seasickness, and even in the wind they run around as if nothing were the matter. It is very sad to see the ladies. For two days not one of them came out on deck. At last they crawled out, but then they had to lie down as soon as they became the least bit seasick. However when the weather is good, you should see how they promenade about the deck. The men take the ladies by their arms as if they were going to dance, and move shakily around the deck.

There is plenty to eat, but it is terrible. At 8:00 AM, tea; at 12:00, lunch, which is really breakfast with soup and pastry; at 4:00, dinner; at 8:00 tea; and at 9:00, supper. But it is honestly all quite dreadful. There are 350 passengers. I am going to stop writing because two young ladies across from me are playing cards with someone, and they are chattering like magpies so that my ears ache, and it is quite impossible to write in my cabin. So, on to Boston . . .

24 August/5 September 1860

When I stopped writing yesterday, we were just approaching Cape Race in Newfoundland. A telegraph line has been constructed here which connects with the United States. A small sloop came up to us, and without stopping we tossed her a tin box with newspapers in it which we had brought from England. All the news will immediately be transmitted to the United States by telegraph, and thus today all of America will know what is happening in

CIVIL AND SAVAGE ENCOUNTERS

Europe. I will send you this letter from Halifax where we should land tomorrow afternoon if conditions are favorable; we will stop there five or six hours. From Boston I will send you word of my arrival in America, probably Saturday evening. After that I will write you from New York. Please realize that my letters will be coming to you more and more seldom. The trip from New York to England takes 12 to 14 days, and it is another 5 or 6 days from England to St. Petersburg; the farther away I am, the more difficult it will be to send letters.

Time passes rather quickly aboard ship. The Americans whom we have met appear generally very obliging and courteous. We have been quite well acquainted with some, and we talk a good deal. Some of the ladies seem to be fond of singing, so a group of us gathers together in the large saloon to sing each evening until about 11:00; we also play chess and other games; then everyone goes to bed in order to meet again at the tea table at 8:00 the next morning. I read a good deal in my free time, since I have brought a good selection of books along. Later when I am on Sitka my letters will assume a different character. From there I will be telling you about everything I have seen, and I will give you my impressions.

For now, until Halifax.

25 August/6 September 1860

We are in Halifax.
On to Boston.

Boston   28 August/9 September 1860

As soon as I had finished penciling my last letter to you, my dear Maman and soeur P., I posted it in Halifax so that it would go out to Europe that same day on the ship *Aravia*, whose signal rockets were soon seen. Now I will tell you about our stay in Halifax. Fog forced us to stay at sea for several extra hours, so we did not dock in the Halifax harbor until 5:00 p.m. At 5:30 I set foot on American soil for the first time. Halifax belongs to England, but one is much aware of the visible change from the Old World to the New. The city is not large; it is built rather like an amphitheater because of the slope of the hills. Many structures, especially in the outlying areas, are built of wood. One sees few negro men, but there are negro women everywhere; they are very unattractive and slovenly, and wear crinolines.

We went ashore as a foursome: Kostlivtsov, a French music teacher from New Orleans named Têtedoux, an Italian marble worker from New York named Octaviano Gori, and I. We walked all around the city together, had some ice cream, and then at 8:00 PM returned to the ship, where they were still loading coal and passenger baggage. At that time the *Aravia*, which was out at sea, fired rockets and blue lights. Our ship responded by signalling her that we were ready to leave harbor, and at 10:00 we were under weigh to Boston.

The weather remained very calm, but a dense fog set in shortly after we left Halifax. The fog was so thick you couldn't see a thing two feet away from the ship. It was so damp I became bored walking on deck, so at 11:00 I went to my cabin and a quarter of an hour later I was sleeping like the dead. The next morning as usual I arose at 6:30, completed my toilette and went up on deck. There I learned that at 2:00 AM our ship, sailing in the fog, had run into a merchant schooner which was fishing, and the schooner sank. Fortunately the captain and crew of 12 men were saved. The poor souls were fished out of the water half naked, shivering from the cold and from terror. But the ship went down with all her cargo.

Our passengers were very sympathetic toward the poor men and took up a collection for them; in a short time they took in nearly 100 pounds sterling. They also took up a collection of clothing and linen and other necessities. Our ship's crew also took up a collection, so the poor sailors received a rather substantial sum of money. After dinner one of the passengers, a most distinguished

CIVIL AND SAVAGE ENCOUNTERS

elderly gentleman, made an appropriate little speech and announced how the money would be distributed among the survivors. Our captain is not to blame for the occurrence; he had taken every precaution: the fog horn had been sounding all the time and the lamps had been lighted; but no one saw the schooner until we had hit her.

The fog lasted almost all day Friday, and Saturday morning there was a light rain, but it was calm, and our ship rapidly approached Boston, and at 11:30 we docked in the harbor. At that hour it was absolutely pouring rain, and we had to carry our own baggage and open it for inspection by the local customs officials. Fortunately one of our passengers, a plantation owner from New Orleans named Blk., was with us the whole time, and he talked with the customs officials so that we were not asked to open our baggage. When we left the customs house we had our trunks put on a carriage and we sat inside. This carriage resembles our old *izvoshchik* [a fiacre], only it is well made and easy to drive. Three men can sit on the back and front seats, and between them under their feet a bench is fitted in, which can seat three more persons, so that in all nine passengers can be seated. It is true that you can't move; I think herring in a barrel have more room. But the coach had a pair of good horses so that in a relatively short time the nine passengers and all their luggage were delivered to their destinations. It is remarkable what an enormous number of trunks, suitcases, bags and other luggage can be put on such a vehicle.

A few *sazhens* from the customs house our carriage stopped at the shore, and then went onto a ferry which in a moment took us across the wide bay to Boston. We did not have to get out of the carriage, nor did the driver get down from his seat. Soon our driver stopped at the entrance of Tremont House, the best hotel in Boston. They immediately gave us extremely pleasant fine rooms. Each of us pays $2.50, about three silver rubles, which includes service. You may eat as much as you wish. In the morning, for example, at tea you can order steak, chops, et cetera, however many things you wish. Precisely the same is true for evening tea. One pays extra for wine. This price is the same in all the best hotels in America, and no one may charge more than that. Hotels here are somewhat different from our European hotels. It is assumed that everyone is responsible for taking care of himself, and therefore you have service only when you ring for it. In the evening when you retire you put your boots outside the door, and in the morning the chambermaid comes in to make up your room. All the rooms have gas light; when you enter you strike a match, hold it up to the gas jet, and your room lights up like a dance hall. There are gas lights everywhere, on the stairs, in the hallways, and thanks to all the soft carpets one does not even hear footsteps in the corridors. Tremont House has more than 200 rooms, both large and small. There is a very large dining room where everyone who is staying in the hotel gathers, both men and ladies. There are also a reading room, smoking room, men's drawing room, ladies' drawing room, and 12 rooms have private baths. There is a hairdresser and a barber shop, and a place to buy soda and seltzer water and various beverages.

The arrangement of the rooms in the hotel is a little strange because of the hillside location. For example, my room is on the lower level, with the window even with the sidewalk. To reach it I come in to the hotel through the main entrance, go down a long corridor, climb up 25 steps, go along two more long corridors, and then go down 40 steps. We settled ourselves in the hotel, changed our wet clothing for dry, washed and shaved. Then Kostlivtsov, Têtedoux, Blk., and I went to the main dining room for dinner, drank a bottle of champagne in honor of our successful arrival in America, and, then in spite of a light rain (it has been raining here steadily for three weeks), we went out on foot to see the city.

Not far from our hotel there is a park considered to be the best in America; but it cannot compare to our Petrovsk Park. The most noteworthy thing in this park is a huge maple tree surrounded by an iron fence; the independence of the United States was proclaimed under this tree. We were much taken with a little squirrel which leaped out of the tree not more than two steps away from us and calmly began to eat a piece of apple on the grass. We walked along the main streets, but saw no particularly famous

London, August 1860.

buildings. The port and the tremendous amount of activity there are quite interesting. When we returned to the hotel it was already dark. We had tea and went to a theater. They were performing a heart-rending tragedy and a little farce. The audience was delighted with the roaring and bellowing of the actors in the tragedy; the excitement of the spectators was manifested with shouts, name-calling and deafening whistles, which are used here to express the height of approval. One of the principle actors came out and gave a speech to thank the audience for all the flattering response. One actor in the farce was not bad, and he added a little drama to the humor. I am pleased to have seen an example of a local production. The theater itself is not bad and is quite clean.

We had planned to leave Boston today, since Sundays here are days of deadly boredom. People go to church all day long; they even have dinner two hours early so they can go to pray again after dinner. All amusements are closed for the day, and most persons do not work. No one sells spirits except at hotels where foreigners stay. Not too long ago they even wanted to prohibit drinking beer on Sundays, but this resulted in fights and newspaper debates, and the brewers won out. Because of Sunday, even the trains don't run. There is only one train, at 8:00 PM, and since we do not wish to travel by night, we have decided to postpone our departure to New York until tomorrow.

New York   29 August/10 September 1860

When I had finished writing to you, my dear Maman and Soeur P., I went into the common room where Têtedoux appeared and announced that at 6:00 PM there would be a special train for New York. We were gleeful over this piece of news and rushed in to eat and then packed our bags, and by 5:30 we were on the train.

I must tell you that since equality is the fundamental principle here, there are neither first nor second nor third class cars on the trains; all cars are the same. They are about like our second class cars except that they are longer, and each seat is for two persons and has a reclining back, so if you wish to sleep you can be comfortable. This reclining back operates in either direction, so you can always travel facing forward. Inside, the cars have gas lights, but since it was Sunday the gas was not lighted, but instead, they used candles in holders on the walls, as they do on our ships.

They cannot boast that the track to New York is well built. It is winding and the cars are long, so that they are forever jerking from one rail to the other, and sometimes across a rail; but since the train goes so fast, the wheels of the cars cannot jump the rails, so everything is fine until there is an encounter with a cow or a sheep or a pig. They do not have the custom of putting fencing along the tracks here, so livestock often stray onto the track and of course can't manage to get away when the train approaches. For this reason every locomotive has an iron grille in front, which goes right along the rail. The grille picks up any animal on the rails and tosses it far off to the side, of course killing it instantly. Its legs and ribs are all broken, so that when one sees an animal that has met this fate, one can never tell just what kind of animal it was—a cow, pig, horse, or simply an assortment of broken bones, hide and meat.

Our steeplechase continued; we had to stop for a train coming from New York, so instead of arriving at 2:00 AM, it was 4:00; by 4:30 we were at the Fifth Avenue House. All the rooms were occupied, so we had to wait until 6:00 when several travelers departed and created a vacancy for us. My room is excellent and is only $2.50 per day, including food. Meals are served from 6:30 AM until 10:00 PM.

Nowhere in Europe are there such hotels as in America. The luxury, neatness and comfort are all exceptional. I can have a bath any day without leaving my hall. I can go downstairs into the hands of the barber. There are all kinds of shops. All rooms have gas, and there is an electric telegraph. Service is immediate. Everything is done instantly, with no grimaces or laziness. Rooms and halls are remarkable, enormous, with all comforts. One need not even ask for anything because it is all at hand. I did not go to bed, just had a

CIVIL AND SAVAGE ENCOUNTERS

bath, shaved, dressed, and at 10:30 Kostlivtsov and Blk. and I set out to see the city.

Ye gods, but it is spread out! What buildings! What streets! You walk about, and you simply cannot get your fill of looking. There is no denying that the old world is in many ways far behind the new. Broadway, the main street, is more than three miles long. Out of curiosity we went into Stewart's Store. This one store occupies a whole building, six stories, and they sell everything from ladies' collars to gloves to rich carpets to oilskins—and everything in huge assortment. You can choose from a thousand things. They took us through the whole store. We also went into hotels, and all of them are similar to the one we are staying in. There were crowds of people everywhere. Carriages crowded along the streets two deep, one behind another, so that it is very difficult to cross from the sidewalk on one side to the other. We hurried off to the post office, and from there went to see our banker to exchange money, and then we dragged back to the hotel, so weary we could barely lift one foot after the other. However this will not prevent us from going to an Italian opera today, and hearing *The Barber of Seville.*

I am writing these few lines while I wait for dinner. I will tell you about the rest of my adventures here before I leave for California.

Washington   3/15 September 1860

In my last letter to you, my dear Maman and Soeur P., I described our arrival in New York. Now I shall continue my tale. On Tuesday morning, August 30, we went to our banker, gave him our letters to be sent to St. Petersburg, and from then until dinner time we walked around the city. I believe I have already mentioned to you that dinner is served here from 5:30 until 7:00. Then one has just enough time to smoke a cigar if one plans to go to the theater, because the opera begins at 8:00. Since we had no obligations that evening, Kostlivtsov, Blk. and I went to the opera, in spite of the rain and the cold.

The theater is very fine, well kept up, but at the moment the artists are rather poor. These are apparently substituting until the regular artists arrive. They performed *Il Trovatore*. Wednesday morning we went off sightseeing again, and that evening we went back to the opera and heard *I Puritani*. Mlle. Patti was quite good. She is still a young singer, but she has a fine voice and sings well, and if she works at it, she may become an outstanding singer. The tenor and the bass, however, were absolutely terrible. It is too bad that Formes, who sang here last season, is no longer here.

When we returned from the theater we saw a procession on the street, with music, torches, and lights with decorated signs. This was a demonstration on behalf of a man named Douglas, whom North American states are voting for as president. The term of office of the present president ends the last of October, so everyone is involved with the election of a new president. Each political party chooses its own candidate, and in order to win more votes for him, it organizes demonstrations for him, arranges meetings, prints articles in newspapers, so that whichever one outdoes the other wins.

Slavery has been abolished in the northern states, but still exists in the South. The North wants to eliminate slavery throughout the Union. The South demands that slavery continue as it is. The northerners, who are known as Abolitionists, are voting for Douglas, also an Abolitionist. The southerners are voting for Bell and Hamlin, who are conservatives. In short, there is fearful commotion; processions are endless; but all will end on the first Monday of November when the president will be elected by majority vote. We were awakened at 6:00 AM Thursday by music and a demonstration for Douglas; there was a new procession at 8:00 AM, and at 12:00 we left New York for Washington.

First we took a steamer, or really, a floating three-story building. It had everything, a common room, ladies' drawing room, dining room, hairdresser; one could promenade around the entire upper deck. This steamer took us across the mouth of the

Hudson River. The trip lasted more than an hour, and we spent the time dining. The train was waiting for us on the other shore, so the steamer stopped directly in front of the railroad station. We had barely jumped aboard when the train began to move and carried us along at a speed of 70 versts per hour. I must confess the Americans are splendid at building railroads. They do not emphasize magnificence or great comfort, nor do they build stations that look like palaces, but they do select a direct route in order to make the journey as swift as possible. If they encounter a river so wide it would be too expensive or impractical to bridge over, they carry the passengers across on a steamer. When they come to a mountain, they tunnel through it. If there is a wide bay or a shallow lake, they drive three rows of piles, join them with cross-ties, lay rails on them, and the train runs along this bridge almost at water level. If there is a city in the way, they lay tracks right through the middle of the street, and the train continues its rapid transit. They do not bother with railings and fences. When the train enters a town it rings its bell, and everyone has to be careful not to fall in front of the cars. Children play peacefully on the sidewalks, the train runs smoothly along the tracks, and everything is fine.

We secured quite good seats in the car. We sat by a window and started to converse, in Russian naturally. Suddenly an older man of about 60 came up to us and started to talk to us in rather poor Russian. Remembering how careful one must be in making acquaintances in this country, we responded politely but rather coolly. Gradually, however, we began to converse. We learned that he is a native of Riga; his name is Adler; he left Russia about 30 years ago and works as a banker in New Orleans. It was 6:00 PM when we reached Philadelphia, and since it takes another six hours to go to Washington, we decided to spend the night in Philadelphia. Adler offered to show us around the city, and in fact he went everywhere with us, acted as our interpreter in the hotel, and was a most helpful and agreeable guide. The next day he put us into a carriage and sent us to the railroad station. He did all of this for us as his fellow countrymen who were unfamiliar with this country. Truly, we were greatly indebted to him.

During this trip I had a slight contretemps. When we left New York, we checked all our things in the hotel and took only the most necessary items with us. I put all of my linen in a small suitcase and also my black dress trousers, but I put the rest of my full dress suit in Kostlivtsov's suitcase which was large enough so that my suit would not wrinkle. Thus our only luggage was Kostlivtsov's suitcase, his traveling bag, and my small suitcase. In Philadelphia, before I went to bed, I picked up my small suitcase in order to get something from it, I tried the key, but it didn't fit. I looked at the name tag on the suitcase, and realized that it was Kostlivtsov's, which was identical to mine, and which we had intended to leave in New York. In our rush to leave, my suitcase remained in New York, and Kostlivtsov's came with us. Thanks to this mix-up, I had no linen, no trousers, and I had to meet with our minister in Washington. I immediately wired New York to send my suitcase to Washington, and I bought a new shirt in Philadelphia. But when we arrived in Washington that evening, my suitcase still had not come. There was nothing to do but to go out and buy new trousers, new boots, new gloves, handkerchiefs and shirts; the whole episode cost me $25, which is about 30 silver rubles. And then the suitcase arrived on the next train just after we came back from seeing our minister. After this I will be more careful . . .

Some time ago in Petersburg there was a rumor that they were thinking of building a horsedrawn railroad along Nevskii Prospekt to transfer heavy goods from the stock exchange to the Moscow road; some persons said it would be impossible because the rails would interfere with carriages, and that accidents would happen with drivers and pedestrians falling down under the cars, et cetera. Here in America almost all the streets in the cities have rails, sometimes two or three rows of them. Enormous cars, pulled by two or four horses, move at a gallop from one end to the other carrying people, and accidents almost never occur. Perhaps this is because the driver guides the horses with one hand, and holds on to the brake handle with the other. A single movement of his arm is enough to stop the wheels, so the car comes to an instant halt. Similar rails have been laid for heavy wagons, and even for simple carriages; all conveyances move on the rails, swinging to the side whenever they encounter a rail car.

After our overnight stay in Philadelphia we proceeded on via Baltimore and reached Washington at 6:00 PM. The next morning, Saturday, we met with out minister, [Edouard de] Stoeckl, who received us in an especially warm fashion and invited us to his home for dinner the following day. Afterward we looked around the city, and in the evening wrote letters . . .

5/17 September 1860

Yesterday at 1:00 PM we went to discuss business with Stoeckl. When we had finished our official business, Stoeckl ordered a light, four-seat cabriolet, and took us to see the various parts of the city. Stoeckl himself drove the horses, Kostlivtsov sat next to him, and I sat in back with [Valdemar] Bodisko, the first secretary of the embassy. The suburban areas are lovely because of the hilly landscape, and this little excursion gave me great pleasure. At 5:30 we returned to Stoeckl's for dinner. We were joined by an artillery colonel, also Russian, and we passed the time until 9:00 PM very pleasantly.

Stoeckl gave us a letter to our consul in New York, asking him to give us a letter of introduction to the captain of the ship we are to take to California, and also requesting him to give us special attention. We have received similar letters to ships' captains from our banker. We have reservations for 9/21 September, but since the ship has no cabins for just two persons, only cabins for three or four or more, we have reserved a three-person cabin for the two of us; we will have to pay for the extra space, but at least we will be more comfortable and have more privacy. Each ticket to California includes meals and costs $250, which is about 300 silver rubles.

Our discussions with Stoeckl indicate that we will have to change our route and return to Russia not via Siberia, but back by way of California and Europe. With these instructions, we will probably be in Russia earlier than we had anticipated. If we reach

Sitka by the end of October, we will be able to travel to the main Aleutian Islands before December; we may start our return journey in January; we will be in New York in March; by the end of May or early June we will be back in Petersburg. There is no point in speculating about the future, however, and you must not worry if you don't receive a letter from me for quite some time. It takes two and a half months for a letter to go from California to Petersburg, and even longer from Sitka. So be patient, and have faith in kind Providence!

You can see that so far our trip is going very well. I am never bored, but it is a little irritating to have to drag our suitcases around all the time. One has to do everything for himself here; servants only clean one's boots, and everyone has to do everything else for himself, as best he can. This is true with railroad journeys, too: no one concerns himself about you. You just ask where you should go, which car to sit in; if you don't ask, no one will pay any attention to you. You simply have to become accustomed to this, and at first, especially for someone who doesn't know the language, it's very difficult. I would like to see how some pampered nobleman, accustomed to being surrounded by servants and never lifting a finger, would come to grips with this situation here. How would he react if, for instance, his bootmaker brought in his boots to measure him, and came right into his room without taking off his hat, and nonchalantly sat down until he had taken the measurements for boots? That is the way it is here. And usually when you go out to an inn, the waiter will put your food in front of you, and then just go off and sit down and read a newspaper until you have finished eating. At first this seems very strange to us, but we have become accustomed to it, and now it is the usual pattern.

At 3:30 this afternoon we will return to New York; we will probably spend the night in Philadelphia, and reach New York the next day at dinner time. I will continue my letter from there.

8/20 September 1860

Everything went as planned. I has just finished writing when Stoeckl arrived and spent an hour with us. In spite of the fact that his title is Envoy Extraordinary and Minister Plenipotentiary, he came on foot, wearing a gray coat and a straw hat, and he had a cigaret in his mouth, like an ordinary citizen of the United States. I find this simplicity extremely appealing.

At 3:30 PM we left Washington, and were in Philadelphia by 7:00. We stayed there overnight. At 9:00 PM there was a huge parade on the street, with torches and music, and the marchers wore red hats. The procession stopped just opposite our hotel, and someone spoke to the people for about three quarters of an hour; then they started up the music and beat the drums, and the procession moved along through the city.

At 11:00 AM the next day we continued on our journey, and were in New York by 3:30. This time, on Stoeckl's recommendation, we stayed at the Clarendon Hotel. It is also beautifully run, but there are not as many people staying there as in some of the other hotels. That evening we went to hear *La Traviata*. Mlle. Cortesi sang quite well, but she is too stout to play the role of a tubercular woman. The opera was staged in a summer theater called Niblo's Garden. The theater is good, but there are few reserved seats, and since we arrived too late for those, we had to stand during the performance.

Yesterday morning we went to our banker and he gave us our tickets to California. tomorrow, 9/21 September, we will go at noon to board the steamer *North Star*, which called at Kronstadt in 1853. I inspected her at that time, and wrote an article on her for *Morskoi Sbornik*, never dreaming that this star would someday in the future carry me from New York to Aspinwall in the Isthmus of Panama. Our cabin is on the upper deck, with good ventilation and plenty of space. We paid $650 for it, which is about 815 silver rubles. Our banker took us to the ship, and on the way we bought straw hats for ourselves and a chest to store our books and cigars and things.

In the evening we went to the banker's for tea. He lives on the other side of the Hudson River, which as I have already written to you, is very wide. If bridges had been built across it, they would have impeded the sailing ships which now dock along shore all around the city. Therefore communication between New York and towns on the far side of the river is by ferry. Carriages go directly on board the ferries, into a covered corridor, which has cabins for ladies and gentlemen along both sides, and buffets, etc. In the evening everything is lighted by gas. It takes only a few minutes to reach the other side of the river.

The banker lives in a very fine home built in the American style. Homes here are generally narrow and tall, so that each is several stories high. The banker's kitchen is on the lower level; the dining room and study are above it; the living room is one more story up; bedrooms are on the uppermost floor. One has to become accustomed to the constant trips up and down the stairs. Candles are rarely used in the homes, because everything is lighted with gas. Even the dining room lamps use gas, which is of excellent quality, with no odor, and is preferred to any other means of illumination. The banker's wife was born in Petersburg, and since we were unaware of this we were very surprised when she began to speak to us in Russian. She is a lovely lady. She and her husband lived in Mexico for several years. Fighting went on constantly while they were there, and on three occasions she found herself in besieged towns. We returned home that evening at 11:00.

The next letter you receive from me will probably be from Aspinwall, but it will not reach you for some time. Last evening when we went down Broadway, the main street, we passed 103 carriages—isn't that amazing? And we didn't even go all the way down the street . . .

New York   8/20 September 1860

When I finished my letter to you today, my Maman and Soeur P., I sent it off to our banker; then Kostlivtsov and I went to see our consul, Notbeck, to give him the letter from Stoeckl requesting him to see to it that we have good accommodations on the ship and are given special attention during our voyage. Such a letter is invaluable where there are 500 passengers from all over on the ship. We did not meet the consul, but his secretary said that he had been holding a letter for me all week. It was your letter from Reval, dated 4 August. It apparently took about a month to go from Reval to New York, which is rather quick. Yesterday a steamer arrived from Europe, probably carring mail for California, which will go along with us on the *North Star*. It is entirely possible that your letter addressed to me in San Francisco will travel with us, and that I will not receive it until we reach there.

It rained all last night, and there was a thunderstorm this morning, and in between, it was so hot that after a trip to see the consul and walk down Broadway and a breakfast of 24 oysters, I returned to the hotel as wet as a drowned mouse. On the way I bought several books, including a Bible in French. I am writing this letter to you while I wait for dinner, and I still have three-quarters of an hour to wait because dinner is served in this hotel at 5:30. It is very interesting to observe everyone gathered around the common table. First of all from 7:00 AM to 10:00 there is tea—the first toilette for the ladies. Anyone who wishes to have tea or breakfast or dinner or supper served in his room must pay an extra charge. Consequently unless one is ill everyone gathers in the common dining room at the appointed hour. Then from noon until 2:00, luncheon, that is to say breakfast, is served—and the second toilette for the ladies. Then a stroll along Broadway—the third toilette. At 5:30, dinner—and the fourth toilette. Then evening tea from 8:00 PM until 10:00; supper from 10:00 until 12:00. Everyone here has become accustomed to this routine, which does not confine anyone, and I understand that it is possible to fit oneself into this schedule.

But there are certain things to which I am quite unable to become accustomed: for example, most of the men, who call themselves gentlemen, chew tobacco and spit revoltingly. There are huge spitoons everywhere, but in spite of this, they are forever spitting on the floors, which have to be washed several times a day. There are marble floors here everywhere. Of course there are carpets in some rooms, and the gentlemen spit into containers of sand. Another habit Americans have is to sit with their feet up, so that if you walk along in front of a hotel and look in the windows you see a great number of feet propped up on the window sills or against the panes, but not a single head. Heads are usually hidden by newspapers.

But there is also much that is good. It would not be a bad thing if our gentlemen adopted some habits and customs from the Americans. There are many many obsolete customs in Europe, which in spite of an affected polish are based on outdated foundations. Here in America everything is new and is constantly moving forward. I understand that once a person becomes accustomed to certain peculiarities of life here, it is possible to become attached to it and to settle here for good. However I am not certain our stomachs could adapt to American cuisine. Stoeckl, who has lived here many years, has almost become an American, but he still keeps a French chef.

At sea, aboard *North Star*   11/23 September 1860

My last two letters to you, my dear Maman and Soeur P., should have been sent from New York yesterday; you will probably receive them by the time this letter reaches you; I am at sea now, and will mail this from Aspinwall.

The last day of our stay in New York was not altogether felicitous. It rained all day from early in the morning, so it was hard to find a good time to make several last minute purchases. On Friday, 9/21 September, we packed, and by 11:00 AM we were aboard the *North Star*. Our cabin is on the upper deck, and is well ventilated, so that we will not suffocate there during the hot weather. And since we paid for the extra berth, there is plenty of room. the only problem is that the berths are built three-high, and are close together, so that if you are restless at night you are likely to hit your head. In general I would have to say that the ship does not live up to our expectations. It is true that she sails well and the engine is quiet, but there is little order, and the food is skimpy and poor. At 7:30 ᴀᴍ there is an inadequate tea, with poor ham, bad butter and a few other such little delicacies. At 1:30, dinner, which is also anything but appetizing; and then at 5:30, evening tea. The rest of the time one has to go hungry because one cannot even buy anything to eat. Furthermore, everything is served in such disorder that I have to carry a clean cloth with me to wipe off the utensils. Of course I laugh at all of this, and submit to circumstances, but Kostlivtsov is furious, and on top of everything else he is seasick all the time in spite of the fact that the weather is beautiful. Frankly, since they charge $225 per person (one dollar=1.25 silver rubles), they really should keep things in better order. Of course there are such a lot of people on board. In all three classes there are about 800 passengers.

We were no sooner aboard the steamer than we met Gr., our old acquaintance and fellow passenger from Liverpool, whom I have already mentioned to you. He is also going to California on business, and he has two young sons with him, whom we also met on the voyage from Europe. Thank God there is at least one familiar face, because it is difficult to make friends here. The words of Pushkin apply quite aptly to our passengers:

> What motley dress and faces,
> Tribes, dialects, stations in life.
> From huts, from cells, from dungeons,
> They have thronged together for gain.

God only knows where they have all come from. There are two or maybe three respectable-looking men, a few ladies, and the devil only knows what the rest are. In third class there are persons the likes of which it would be unpleasant to meet at night on the street. Yet it is all very understandable. Certain swindlers, who abound in the northern states and are pursued by police, are rushing off to California with the help of their friends, in hopes of improving their condition there. Third class is separated from us by a barrier, but we still lock the doors of our cabin tight in order to keep some poor Yankee from temptation. I don't even put my boots outside the door at night to be cleaned, for fear they will end up on the feet of someone from the other side of the barrier. There is one more annoyance, and that is the tremendous number of children of both sexes and all ages who constantly run around on deck, knock you down, drop chairs on your legs, and shout so much that your ears ache.

The proprietor of the buffet is an old negro; his wife is also a negro, a real *panier à charbon* and wears a crinoline and silk clothing. Our captain is completely uncouth scarecrow with a reddish beard and an ugly red face. There are two or three young ladies who are not bad; one reminds me amazingly of Arsn., Mpl.'s former adjutant, whom you met in my quarters; but she rarely comes up on deck because she suffers so much from seasickness that she is always lying down in her cabin. The heat is becoming quite oppressive, and if it crescendoes, tomorrow I shall dress like a canary in my summer costume.

14/26 September 1860

At 8:00 AM today we sighted the island of Cuba. After three more days at sea we will reach Aspinwall. In the meantime, everything is still the same: the food is bad, the children raucous, and I don't know why they have chosen the exact part of the ship where my cabin is located for their playground. To all this, add the very intense heat which increases every day. I have arrayed myself in my summer costume, but nevertheless I am constantly soaking wet, and at night I swelter in spite of the fact that we open both windows in the cabin for cross ventilation. Still, I am not bored, and because of my own idiosyncrasies I am even becoming accustomed to this life. Sometimes there are diverting incidents. Last evening, for example, the sky was covered with dense clouds; there was lightning in the distance, and one could hear thunder. But the sea was calm, and the foamy wake of the ship was agleam with phosphorescent sparkles. On deck, by the glow of the lamp, several ladies and their partners were dancing the polka and

CIVIL AND SAVAGE ENCOUNTERS

lanciers [quadrilles] to the music of a poor violin! A big circle of onlookers surrounded the dancers, and everyone was happy, carefree, in a joking mood; no one thought to look at the distant danger, nor did anyone realize that in a single moment this joy could change into shock and horror. I watched the storm and the dancers for a long time, and thought a great deal about the past, the future, my far-off homeland, and friends whom I have left for a long time . . . . Well, I hope I will find your letters in California, but I will have to wait a long time for that . . . .

16/28 September 1860

In a few more hours we will be in Aspinwall. So far everything has been going extremely well, and if you receive this letter it will mean that the rest of the passage was successful. I am hurrying to finish writing this letter, because we will arrive in Aspinwall tomorrow morning between 11:00 and 12:00, and the letter must be ready then, and it is now 8:00 in the evening. Frankly, it would be difficult to have a better voyage than ours. We have not had a single strong wind the whole time, the sea has been very calm, and the wind has always been favorable. It is true that some persons, including Kostlivtsov, have been seasick, but other than that everything has gone very well. The poor food has affected a few of our passengers to some extent, but thank God I am healthy, perhaps because I have been eating a great deal of potatoes and roast beef, and drinking nothing but cold water mixed with red wine.

During our voyage we have gradually found several of our fellow passengers who speak French. Among them are two ladies, a mother and her daughter. The former is about 40, and the latter is about 17 and not bad looking. I still do not know their surname, but from what the mother says I gather that her husband is a gunsmith in San Francisco. I chat with these ladies all the time now, and time passes quickly in conversing with them and in reading. Kostlivtsov's voyage is not at all like mine. It is true he also converses with the ladies, but since his French is not very good, and his German is even worse, and he does not speak a word of English, and on top of all that he is seasick, it is no wonder that he is depressed over his sea voyage. He is forever asking each and every person whether there is not some way to travel back from San Francisco to New York overland, and he is forever receiving a most unsatisfactory reply. He is even ready to decide to return by way of Siberia.

Of course it would be very interesting to see Siberia, but the journey via New York would be shorter in the first place, and in the second place *I am obligated* to meet with our envoy, Stoeckl, upon my return, unless some important circumstance should intervene. Therefore I have resolved that at all costs I will try to return by the same route. I will not see Siberia, but I will carry out fully the assignment that has been given to me. In general, however, I get along well with my companion, and I trust that there will be no cause for disagreement in the future. At least this is how I am conducting my affairs.

I will write my next letter to you from San Francisco, and we will see how things go. Everything will depend on whether the ship which is to take us to Sitka is there. At any rate, I plan to travel to Sacramento and to the gold fields. This can be done very quickly by ship, and they say that it is very interesting. I am going to buy two cotton coats for myself in Aspinwall. Although I have full dress clothes from Petersburg, this does not seem appropriate because of all the dirt on the ship.

Steamer *Washington*, in
Tuantepec Bay   27 September/9 October

I sent you my last letter from Aspinwall, my dear Maman and Soeur P. I daresay it will reach you in due time, and so I will continue describing my trip. On 17/29 September we reached Aspinwall about noon, but here we had our first disappointment.

New York City. One of that city's entertainment halls.

The steamer *Stephenson*, which was to pick us up in Panama and take us to San Francisco, did not arrive on time. They assume that something has happened to her and that she may have been forced to return to San Francisco, or perhaps she may even have been wrecked. In any case, up to the present time nothing has been heard of her whereabouts. Since local ship companies do not have the practice of taking accidents into account, the emergency ship has been sent to some place in South America, and the only vessel left in Panama is an old steamer, *Washington*, which has not been used at all for more than six months. She has been without cargo, uncared for, engine partly dismantled, without crew, officers, or even a skipper. They immediately began to get this old ark ready, and informed us that we would have to stay in Aspinwall for a day or two.

The prospect of life in such a little town as this did not appeal to us at all, and consequently we requested that they take us at least to Panama where everything is a bit better than in Aspinwall. But to our misfortune, the Panamanians have had the wild idea of having a revolution. The Liberals or negroes and the Conservatives or whites have quarreled among themselves, and although the Conservatives gained the upper hand and expelled the Liberals from the town, sailors from English and American ships took up posts at the railroad station. It was learned that we would not be welcome even to poke our noses into the city, which was under siege, so we were forced to stay in Aspinwall. There is nothing to do.

Kostlivtsov and I, and a certain Madame Laguarde and her daughter, two Mexican-Germans, Gr. with children and another young German, Dol., ordered several negroes to carry our luggage on their backs, and we moved through the unbearable heat to the Hotel St. Charles, which fortunately is located not too far from the harbor. They gave out the rooms by putting several persons in each room, at $3 per person per day, including meals but not wine. We found our rooms infested with rats, red cockroaches, ants and mosquitoes. You can imagine how pleased I was in such company! To all of this, add a great amount of dirt, and the unbearable stench from constantly sweating negroes and from the swamps that surround the city, and you will have some understanding of our bliss.

Actually, Aspinwall is not a town, but a row of poor hotels built one right next to another. There are a few small shops and taverns, and in front of everything is the railroad track; beyond that, there is the Atlantic Ocean on one side, and endless swampland on the other. We had to spend two days in this blessed town. Fortunately our little group was cheerful, so that during the daytime when the heat was too great for us even to put our noses out on the street, we locked ourselves up in the general room and chatted, ordering vast quantities of ice water mixed with red wine. In the evening when the heat subsided we went out as a group to walk around the town in areas that were safe.

I had imprudently brought too little summer clothing, so I had to buy several readymade things in Aspinwall. I soon found light cotton goods, but as for a waistcoat—that's another story. The proprietor of the store was boasting about his waistcoats, and took a carton from the shelf. There actually were waistcoats inside, but they had been chewed up by rats, and furthermore there was a whole nest of baby rats which had just come into God's world. So we managed to make do in Aspinwall, eating very little and only treating ourselves to fruit.

In two days they told us we could at last depart for Panama. At noon on 19 September/1 October the railroad car stopped in front of our hotel, and three hours later we were in Panama. We went straight to the harbor, where a small steamer was to take us to the celebrated *Washington*. But here there was another little delay, the tide had gone out, and the ship could not come into harbor before high tide, which was about four hours later. There was nothing to do, so we took off on foot into Panama, perched in some sort of eating place and ordered breakfast. Fortunately the breakfast seemed better than any of the dinners which they had served us aboard the steamer *North Star* or in Aspinwall. Finally at about 6:00 they put us aboard the ship,

CIVIL AND SAVAGE ENCOUNTERS

and an hour later we disembarked onto the *Washington,* which was anchored at one of the small islands located in the roadstead.

Panama, which some time ago blossomed under Spanish control, is now in complete decay. It is a pile of tumbledown dwellings of stone and wood. A large part of the population is negro. We saw one negro here, a red republican, who had painted himself with red paint, not only the top of his straw hat, but his shirt and trousers and legs. The negro men and women generally are not very good looking, they are dirty, and their children walk around completely naked, without even the tiniest fig leaf.

Well, we finally went aboard *Washington.* She is a huge old tub, extremely ungainly, sluggish and dirty. The captain was recruited from one of the naval vessels; the crew and servants have been picked up from wherever they can be found; some are negroes, some are from naval vessels. Fearful chaos. Fortunately the captain appears to be very much in command and is efficient; however it is difficult to have only three days to prepare a ship for a long voyage when she has been a complete derelict for several months.

On the afternoon of 20 September/2 October we finally raised anchor and sailed at a speed of six knots per hour on our further voyage. We have no sails at all. There were some old ones, but they were rotten. The engine is rusty but it works, not fast, but well enough. But we cannot protect ourselves from the filth and chaos. Kostlivtsov and I fell heir to a cabin on a lower deck, not bad, but although it has a rather large porthole, it is so hot that at night we wear the same costume as the little negro children. During the daytime for the most part we are up on deck. At 9:00 AM they serve tea and breakfast, that is to say a tasteless brew and beefsteak that breaks one's teeth, fried pork that causes indigestion, and ham in which there is more salt than meat. Then at 12:00 we have lunch (hence the expression "to lunch"), a few pickles, two or three sardines and preserves. You recall how much I like preserves? Well, here I judiciously obliterate them with white bread. At 5:00 PM—dinner: turbid water for soup, old beans, green asparagus in grease, rice, fried pork and sweet cakes made with vegetable oil.

This concludes our daily menu, and we go to sleep on an empty stomach. Thus in spite of the fact that I constantly carry a supply of biscuits in my pocket, I am always as ravenous as a wolf, and I lose ¾ of a pound every day. At least, when I went aboard ship there was nothing to do and so I weighed myself, and found that I weighed 143 pounds. Three days later I weighed 140½. How will we fare after 20 days, which is the least it takes the dear old *Washington* to reach San Francisco?

My second torture—the children who are constantly running about, singing and shouting—this is real punishment. I have already considered throwing some of them overboard, the ones who shout the most, in order to discover whether or not they know how to swim. Their mothers would not miss them, because most of them will be giving birth again in a short time. *Cette couvée d'enfants est vraiment un cauchemar.* But God forgive them all! Then there are the servants: barefoot, unclothed, dirty beyond belief, inexperienced and rude. After that, the filth, ever present blobs of tobacco spittle all over the whole deck, and in the large cabin the floor is covered with so much dirt and grease that one can slip on it and break one's nose. On top of all this, the sun is so hot that day and night you sweat incredibly, and go around all the time like a drowned rat. Fortunately there is ice on the ship, and this helps a little to quench the thirst.

Today it is exactly one week since we put to sea, and we are sailing in a continual calm. They have promised that tomorrow toward evening we will reach the little port of Acapulco where we will take on coal. It would be nice if they would also take on some provisions. They say that there is a decent little hotel in Acapulco. We are just waiting for the moment when we finally reach this promised land and eat something more appetizing than old shoe leather, which we are presently consuming in the guise of beefsteak. However, except for these vicissitudes, time passes rather quickly for me, with books and conversation with the French ladies and with the Germans. As far as Kostlivtsov is concerned, he is cursing the day he was born, and swears that nothing in the world will make him agree to make the return voyage aboard American ships.

At sea   2/14 October 1, 1860

It happened just as we supposed. Thursday night, 28 September/10 October, we came to the Acapulco roadstead, and since there are no lighthouses to indicate the channel, on the first attempt the bow of our ship came to rest on the sand, where we remained until morning. This did not prevent a multitude of little boats with fruit and all other kinds of things from coming out to the ship. Tired from the heat of the day, and unable to do anything because of the dim light and the heat, I changed into Adam's costume, and by 10:00 I was in a deep sleep, of course as wet as if I'd just been pulled out of the water. I was up on dock by 5:00 AM. Imagine the deck strewn with a deep layer of orange and banana peels from one end to the other, wet from the night rain, and a whole anthill of men, women and children buying fruits, shellfish, wine, et cetera, from the native boats—it was marvelous chaos!

I hurried to join our group, that is, Madame Laguarde and her daughter, a Spaniard, Don Pedro de Rumeiro, and Kostlivtsov; and the five of us boarded a native boat and sailed to shore. I must tell you that the Germans who were in our group, Kuehn and Jacobs, found a small boat in Acapulco which may get them to their appointment several days ahead of us; therefore they have decided not to go with us to San Francisco, and they took leave of us last night. As for Don Pedro de Rumeiro, he is a wholesale cigar merchant from Havana, a good friend of Madame Laguarde's husband, and appears to be a very fine person. So the five of us went ashore. The scorching sun had already begun to beat on our heads, but this time we had armed ourselves with parasols and fans.

Acapulco is a little Mexican town of 2,500 or 3,000 inhabitants, mostly negro. When you read the words "little town," you may visualize something on the order of our *uezd* [district] towns, but this is something quite different. Imagine a superb bay surrounded on all sides by high hills. The hills are covered with vegetation. In spite of the fact that they are composed of granite, mighty Nature has garbed them in green. They are covered with shrubs from top to bottom, and in the glens, in places where the soil is somewhat more hospitable, there are towering trees such as palms, coconut palms, lemons, bananas. The entire bay is simply enchanting! It is a superb natural bay, protected by little islands that are quite high. From the sea one can only see cliffs, green on top but barren at sea level. The Pacific Ocean has washed these shores and created the steep inaccessible walls of a natural fortress. The entry to the bay is guarded by a fort. General Santa Ana laid siege to it and could not take it. I walked around it, and in spite of the twenty guns which defend it, and the fact that it has a moat, I would wager that I could seize this stronghold with 150 volunteer sailors. There is a very poor and badly armed 20-gun American corvette in the roadstead.

The town is spread out in the foothills along the shore of the bay. It is really nothing more than a collection of clay-walled cottages. All the homes are built of poles, and have just one story. Some are smeared with clay both inside and out and are then covered with dirt or stucco, but more of them are built just of poles and are not plastered, so that from the street it is possible to see everything that happens in the house. These are the dwellings of negroes who live there with fine pigs, chickens et cetera. The children here do not wear any clothes, either.

When we came ashore we immediately bought 100 eggs and 50 bottles of red wine. Then we presented ourselves in the one *salon* of the Hotel Louisiana, whose proprietress, a stout French woman, received us nicely and immediately cooked a chicken for us, gave us fresh eggs and delicious steaks and good wine. Of course this brought us back to life, and when we had eaten our fill, we went to look at the town and the fort. They would not let us into the fort, but they did allow us to walk around the walls. Mexican guards were on duty in white shirts, white trousers and straw hats; only their weapons and pouches indicate that they are soldiers. I engaged in conversation with an officer who was eating bananas under a fig tree, and who was dressed exactly the same as the soldiers. He talked about the fort, and with total conviction he emphasized the fact that it is impregnable. Of course I did not disillusion him. After our walk we went back to the Louisiana and laid in our reserves against a rainy day. The five of us bought 100 eggs, 50 bottles of wine, several roasted chickens, bread, biscuits and 200 oranges. This is how we are hoping to avoid hunger, so we will not reach San Francisco completely exhausted from hunger and deprivation. Fortunately the *Stephenson*, which we were to have taken from Panama to San Francisco, was not wrecked after all. Forty-five miles out of Acapulco her engine melted, and somehow she reached Acapulco under sail, where her passengers were transferred to the next ship (ten days later), and she proceeded under sail to San Francisco for repairs.

We remained in Acapulco until 2:00 PM 30 September/11 October, when we managed to leave that port. Now we are slowly approaching San Francisco, ripening in the intolerable heat, surrounded by 60 children, at least 59 of whom are superfluous, in my judgment. The heat is so terrible that for 24 hours of the day we are all soaking wet, in the most literal sense of the word. In spite of this I read, chat with passengers in various languages, and the time does pass. There is a great deal to see, both good and bad, if only one could keep from nodding off. I am able to find something good in even the most unpleasant little things, and I am not grumbling. What a clear sky! What a calm and peaceful sea! It would be difficult to have smoother sailing. The ship does not roll, there is total calm, and sometimes I inadvertantly pray God to send a tiny breeze to refresh us, but none comes. Everything is quiet and clear and there is not one breath of wind! . . . Last Sunday I listened to a long sermon given by a Methodist minister. I thought that he might be speaking again today, but unfortunately, or fortunately, he came down with yellow fever and there was no sermon.

Near Cabo San Lucas   4/16 October 1860

I am so much longing to have a talk with you, my dear Maman and Soeur P., but it is hard to find a corner where I can squeeze myself in with some paper. The captain has offered me his cabin, but he is busy there himself, doing mathematical calculations, and I do not want to bother him. So I am writing to you sitting on a bench in the most uncomfortable and unnatural position. Fortunately it is a little cooler today so there is some respite from the heat which has been so oppressive for so long. Other than that, everything is just the same as before, the children are still crying and everything is still dirty, but the food is slightly better. I have already complained to the captain several times about the service and other inconveniences. He keeps assuring me of his readiness to be of service to me personally, and he does not seem to understand that I am not asking for special favors for myself, rather that I am just like the other passengers, and that I am not protesting on my own behalf, but in the name of all the rest of us as well. This seems completely illogical to him. He is ready to do everything possible for me, since I have a letter to him from a representative of the company, but he is not concerned about the other passengers.

I have also noticed that patronage and money always play an important role, even in liberal England. For example, on the train in England smoking is prohibited in the cars, but after we gave the conductor several shillings we smoked all the time. In Belgium we gave the conductor two cigars, and he gave us a car to ourselves. You can get anything with money in America, and without it, you cannot take a step. When I reach Sitka and have a free moment, I will tell you briefly about this much-glorified America, beginning with the United States and including all the republics. I will have to wait until I return to Russia to give you a longer description, because on the return trip I am going to try to gather more detailed and trustworthy information from our envoy and consuls. On the other hand, the food on the ship is much better now. Thanks to a new amateur butcher, who is one of our passengers, the meat is much better and we are not starving as we were before. If there is wind tomorrow we will still manage to reach San Francisco, where my first plan is to have a bath.

10/22 October 1860

We have now been at sea more than a month, starting from New York, and we still do not know whether we will be in San Francisco tomorrow. Our illustrious *Washington* moves like a turtle. And on top of everything else, the firemen who were picked up wherever possible know absolutely nothing, so that the steam often dies out. Friday night we spent four whole hours in one place because there was not enough steam. However, at least now the heat is not so bad. We were scarcely out of the tropics when cold weather set in, so that we had to put on our woolen clothes, and now it is impossible to stay up on deck without a coat or wrap of some kind after the sun goes down. We feel the cold all the more because of the too rapid transition from the unusual heat. This is the fifth day that a north wind has been blowing; there are considerable waves which slow our progress even more. However, we must hope that we will reach our destination at least by dinner time on Wednesday, if not tomorrow night. God willing! It is positively sinister with the present food situation, the dirt, the wet, and especially with the children. Kostlivtsov's constant grumbling infuriates me even more; his groans and wailing do not help the matter a bit, but only bore me to death.

Yesterday there was a mournful ceremony. One of the third-class passengers, who was already ill when she came aboard, died. They sewed her body in a hammock, the captain said a prayer, and then they lowered her body into the water. In addition to this, we have quite a few sick persons. Almost all the passengers who stayed in Aspinwall and in Panama more than a week while they were waiting for our ship became ill with yellow fever, and walk about like shadows, yellow and wasted.

Every day I am more and more amazed by the Americans. They are astonishing people. They are egoists by nature; they love to speculate and are backward in everything else. They are like children, amused by every trifle. If a swallow or some other bird flies by, everyone rushes off to see this wild creature with frantic yells and laughter. Their songs—God only knows what they are!—almost always end with dancing. All the women like to dress up and they are forever walking about in huge crinolines which are finally beginning to irritate me as much as the children do—there is hardly room to pass them on the deck. Well, God willing, perhaps our old tub *Washington* will soon bring us to our destination, and of course I will not be sailing aboard her again when I return to Europe.

When we reach San Francisco I will finish this letter and send it off on the first ship, but it will be delayed somewhat, because the ship that carried the mail has already put out to sea, and the next one will not leave until 31 October, new style. My letters will be coming to you less frequently than before, so do not be surprised if you do not hear from me very often. It takes a letter at least three months to go from Sitka to St. Petersburg. There is no way to avoid this; there will be times this winter when you will be anxious, but then my letters will start coming more frequently.

San Francisco   13/25 October 1860

At last the *speedy Washington* brought us to San Francisco at 9:00 yesterday morning. We all breathed a sigh of relief, and were overjoyed to see the granite rocks of San Francisco. We had just barely docked at the harbor when a man came to the ship, having been sent by [Petr] Kostromitinov, who is the company's agent and our consul here. He suggested that Kostlivtsov and I go off to call on the consul. We left all our things on the ship and pushed our way through a huge crowd of passengers and other persons who had come down to the ship. We worked diligently with our knees and elbows and finally managed to get ashore. We found a carriage and went off to see Kostromitinov. Our intention was to ask him where it would be best for us to stay, and then at his direction, send our luggage to that hotel. But before we even managed to explain our wishes to him, Kostromitinov announced that a room had already been prepared for us at his home, and that he had sent for our luggage.

So we settled in Kostromitinov's house, which belongs to the [Russian] American Company. His wife seems to be a very kind lady, and they have six children. Their oldest son is to be our guide. I am not writing you anything about San Francisco, because I still have not seen the city. I will send you a detailed description in my next letter.

We will not be leaving for Sitka for at least a week and a half, because the *Tsaritsa*, the ship we will be sailing on, will need that much time to unload her cargo and take on a new one.

This morning we opened our trunks. Because of all the dampness, many of our things were covered with mildew, and moss had even grown on our boots. Everything is now being aired out and dried. Well, we made the journey from New York to San Francisco in 33 days, although the usual time is 20 days. Here we do not think about how slow our ship was, but simply thank God that we have arrived. It is really tempting fate to send a ship like *Washington* out to sea to sail almost 2,500 miles without sails, with a rotten mast, an old engine, a crew gathered from all the gutter-sweepings of the earth. By way of justification the Company can only offer the fact that it wished to protect the passengers from yellow fever, which some of us probably would have contracted had we remained long in Panama. This excuse is almost like cutting off one's head to cure a toothache. I am hurrying to finish this letter in order to send it by shore post. In a week another post will go out through Panama, and my next letter to you will go with it.

In my last letter to you, my dear Maman and Soeur P., I described our voyage aboard the *Washington*, and our arrival in San Francisco. The Company ship, *Tsaritsa*, which arrived three days before we did, was to have been ready in a week, so the plan was for us to leave today or tomorrow for Sitka. But since *Tsaritsa* carried a cargo of ice, and is taking flour and other provisions back to Sitka, the unloading has gone very slowly. The loading will also take time, and it appears that it will be 10 days before we leave, which will be 3 November, our old style. We are not bored here, however, and since we will be in Sitka for quite a long time, there is no harm in our spending several extra days here.

We are staying in our consul's home. We each have our own room, and we have dinner and breakfast and tea with his family. His wife is a very nice person, and of their six children, only the four younger ones occasionally quarrel. The oldest son is 14 and there is a daughter of 13; they are both very nice children. The consul offered us meals and lodging in his home without any remuneration, simply as one Russian to another; we agreed to this when we thought we would be here for only a short time; but since we are now staying longer, we have taken this opportunity to insist that he accept $3.50 from each of us per day (about 4.25 silver rubles), which is very inexpensive by local prices. Thus our stay here will not be a burden on the consul, and we are freer.

Now a few words about San Francisco. Ten years ago in the site where the city now stands, there were only a few wooden shacks, the first settlement of miners who were attracted to California because of gold in the Sacramento River. These miners stopped only briefly in San Francisco, where the ships they had come on could find a safe and convenient anchorage, and then they rushed off into the hills in search of gold. But there were also entrepreneurs who realized that they could make a fortune without working in mines or panning for gold. They began to bring provisions into San Francisco, and to build stores and boarding houses. Everything was sold by goldweight; there was no currency of any sort. They bought produce with gold dust, by weight, and they paid for small purchases with a pinch of gold dust. The city began to expand without any formal plan, just as it happened to grow, at first along the shore, then up the sides of the hills. Everyone built just as he pleased. Then the United States annexed California. From this land which was still almost empty, a new state was organized; authorities came; government was set up; the population expanded rapidly. San Francisco grew. Towns also sprang up in other places. I look and can scarcely believe my eyes, that it has been possible to do so much in 10 years.

San Francisco has its own altogether individual character. It is laid out on the hillside along the shore of a rather extensive bay into which the Sacramento River empties. When you enter this bay from the sea, first of all on the right you see a new fort at the very base of a high hill, which has a lighthouse and telegraph on top. When you are just past the fort, in the distance on the right San Francisco is revealed. The view of the hills that surround the bay is rather monotonous. The hills are dun colored, rocky, and have little vegetation. But I am told that on the far side of the hills there are many fine meadows and absolutely magnificent fields. The best indication of the productivity of this area is the fact that livestock here are generally husky and fine and that grain grows in wonderful abundance.

Since agriculture is being developed here, there is no doubt that in a short period of time California will be one of the richest agricultural markets in the world. They are already starting to export wheat from here to Europe in substantial amounts. Steam-driven flour mills work day and night, and each grinds from 2,000 to 3,000 puds* of flour per day. Fruits are superb; most are still brought here from Oregon, but orchards are beginning to be introduced here. I ate local apples and pears which were exceptionally juicy and flavorful, and of enormous size.

The people here are moving earth from the hills to dump into the bay to reclaim land for building harbor facilities which would

---

*One *pud* = 36 pounds.—Eds.

enable ships to come directly into dock to unload. They are building warehouses and stores on this same landfill. Most of the homes are built of wood, and are very handsome and comfortable. They have one or two stories. To be sure, the construction is very light, but it is quite adequate for the climate of the region. On the main streets, especially Montgomery Street, there are five-story stone buildings. In other parts of town there are smaller stone buildings, two or occasionally three stories. They are narrow, but compensate for this by depth. Everything is kept very clean here, and has a unique aspect. I cannot remark on the cleanliness of the streets, which are usually not sprinkled, but stone or board walks have been built everywhere, and gas and water are piped into even the most outlying parts. This has all been done just recently. Earlier all the city officials were thinking only about how to misappropriate as much money as possible from the city revenues, and then run off somewhere in the Atlantic states where they could escape all pursuit.

Gas and water are brought into all the homes. They really could not exist here without that. Gas burns in the restaurants, in hotels, in offices, and at the desks and work tables of our host. This is very fine and convenient, especially with the servant situation here; they are very poorly trained, and there are very few of them because they cost so much. The worst lackey receives $30 (37.50 silver rubles) per month, his own room, meals at his employer's expense, and has his linen washed at the expense of the lady of the house. A female cook who barely understands food has the same benefits and receives from $30 to $35. A seamstress who comes to your home receives her meals and pay of $2.50 to $3.00 per day (3 to 4 silver rubles). For this reason all ladies who have large families have sewing machines, which are wonderful and very useful. There are many of these machines in the United States, and they are improved all the time.

The machines are built to look like a small cabinet or a little worktable. Inside the cabinet there is a flywheel which is easily put into motion by a treadle, just like a spinning wheel. Beside the wheel there are little boxes for needles, thread, et cetera. Below, there is the machine itself. Once the wheel starts moving the machine is put into motion and begins to sew, and then all one has to do is guide the material to be sewn with the hands. With a little practice, it is very simple. In earlier times these machines sewed rather irregularly so that if a thread broke the entire seam would pull apart. This has been corrected now, so that it is easier to rip the material than to tear the seam. With this machine you can sew anyway you wish, up, down, back and forth; you can make any size stitch from very long to very short. You can make ruffles, gather, sew either silk or wool, and use any pattern you wish—and all of this with a speed that is almost unbelievable. Our consul's wife will sit at this machine all day long to make clothing for her six children. She showed us how it operates. For a demonstration she took a piece of cotton about three *arshins* [one *arshin* = 28 inches] long and made a row of stitches along its entire length, and this took her only about half a minute. The stitches were very fine, and were made in a way that would have been quite impossible to duplicate by hand. Right in front of us she sewed a quilted cotton cloth with various designs, with amazing speed. She made a gauzy rose party dress for her daughter, with a bodice, flounces, and various trimmings, all in three-and-a-half hours. I shall have to learn how to operate this machine myself, because my description is not very clear. If it is possible to buy one, then I will learn how to sew and, when I come home, I will teach you, chère Soeur P.

Now, on to more about California. When I look at how homes are built here, I think of Arsn. I think he would be shocked at the construction. It is usually done in this way: they dig down to a certain depth, and lay a brick foundation in the excavation, right on the ground, which is sandy and rocky here. This serves as the basement. When this foundation is raised slightly above ground level, they start building walls on three sides, about a foot and a half thick. For the front facade they place cast iron columns directly on the foundation. Above this they build the second floor, and between the columns they put wide doors and windows, so that the lower floor looks as if it were all glass. Instead of beams they use planks five or six inches thick, about two feet apart, and they nail the flooring on these. The roofs are almost always flat and covered with tin sheets.

Wooden homes are built even more simply. They dig out a little dirt and drive square wooden posts into the four corners; the posts are about six inches thick. They drive in additional posts between these. Then they put upright board about two-and-a-half inches thick on these; then square vertical pillars about four inches thick go on the corner posts, and these are as long as the house is high. Then several more thick boards are placed vertically between the two corner posts, forming a sort of cage. This cage is then covered with boards, both inside and out, and the walls are thus ready. Of course they leave spaces for windows and doors. The floor is nailed to the beams, and then it is finished. A carpenter can put a house like this together in his own yard, and then take only seven or eight days to build it in the desired location. The only thing left to do is to paint the outside, plaster the inside, put down carpets in all the rooms, build a fireplace, add furniture—and move right in. All homes here are built like this. Of course in case of fire, such kindling is fine fuel, but since all the homes are insured and the fire department is well organized, no one gives much thought to this danger.

The city has burned twice, and each time it has been rebuilt more beautifully than before. Now, with improved fire fighting equipment and water hydrants in all the streets, it rarely happens that more than a single house burns. There were four fires during the time we were there, and all were put out in about half an hour, which of course was long enough for one house to burn to the ground.

24 October/5 November 1860

When gold was discovered in California, naturally a great mass of humanity swarmed here from all the corners of the world, all hoping to get rich quick. And of course most of these people were adventure seekers. With all of this you can imagine how these

CIVIL AND SAVAGE ENCOUNTERS

San Francisco's Market Street with Twin Peaks beyond.

people inundated California. The madness for gold seized everyone. They all tried to get it any way possible—and this led to murder, armed robbery, et cetera. Authorities, even elected officials, took part in the pillage and connived with swindlers. But in the meantime law-abiding people gradually began to come in too. The city spread out and was built up, but there was neither order nor security. With a bribe of money a known murderer could be freed from justice and could escape to the Atlantic states or to some other land where there was no possibility of pursuit. People complained, but affairs went on the same way.

Then suddenly a man came who resolved to publish the details of all these abuses. This was the literary figure Williams King [James King of William]. He published a newspaper [*Evening Bulletin*] in which he mercilessly branded all the culprits, named them, presented the facts in support of his accusations. In a short time he acquired a great following among loyal people, but at the same time he infuriated the authorities and a whole group of scoundrels, who tried in every way they could to buy him off. They even tried to frighten him, but he carried on, neither succumbing to bribes nor being frightened by threats. Finally the scoundrels decided to kill him. One day he was on his way home from his office to have breakfast, and as he was crossing one of the main streets, a man ran up to him, saying, "Defend yourself!" and shot him with a revolver. Williams fell, mortally wounded. The people rushed up to the killer and took him to the police. More than 30 men testified as to what had happened. Williams died, and the trial of the killer, [James] Casey, dragged on. Rumors spread throughout the city that Casey's lover, a very rich woman, had paid money to get him out of San Francisco.

The people were incited to the point of rebellion. One day more than 6,000 men gathered at a meeting and elected representatives whom they called the Committee for Vigilance. They immediately armed themselves and moved on to the police station, arrested the police, and seized Casey and several other murderers who were in prison, and brought them to a building where they posted a citizens' guard. Then patrols of these same citizens went all through the city to maintain order, and the Committee immediately tried Casey and the other murderers by legal means. The evidence was all too clear. Casey and one other man [a murderer named Cora] were sentenced to death.

On the day of the journalist Williams' funeral, the supporters of the Committee, consisting of 6,000 armed citizens, lined up on one of the squares and placed their cannon in such a way that by firing they could stop any movement among the people who were gathering in crowds around the square and in nearby streets and buildings. They fastened two horizontal beams on the roof on a building, and the ends of the beams protruded from the roof so as to hang over the windows of the upper floor. They fastened a block and ropes there, and erected a small platform from the two windows that were below the beams. When Williams' coffin was put on the hearse, Casey and the other man condemned to death were brought out to the platform through the window. Nooses were placed around their necks. When the funeral procession started, the supports were knocked out from under their feet, and the murderers spun in the air. They say the effect was a sensation.

The Committee did not stop with this. Patrols constantly went through the city picking up suspects. Many scoundrels were arrested and sentenced; three or four were hanged and the Committee sent the rest, at its own expense, by ship to Australia, the Sandwich Islands, or to the Atlantic states, and warned them not to return to California under threat of death. In this manner order was gradually restored, and the Committee discontinued its activity when new authorities elected by the people took office. Thanks to these measures, one no longer hears about robberies here, and at night one can walk safely along all the streets where it was previously impossible to go unarmed, even in daytime. However, the Committee did not completely disband. It still exists, and at any hint of trouble may again take over. Of course murders are still being committed as a result of fights, quarrels, et cetera but the Committee is not concerned with such matters. A murderer is arrested, tried, hanged, and that is the end of it. Sometimes there are abuses, but this is a result of misuse of the law, and where are there no abuses? Let me tell you about one such case.

A man named [David C.] Broderick, a California senator, aroused the dissatisfaction of the opposition party. Hostility grew greater and greater. Several times Broderick was insulted in various ways, but did not pay any attention. But finally a man named [David S.] Terry insulted him publicly, in such a way that Broderick had to challenge Terry to a duel. At the appointed time the opponents met, and Broderick was killed. Then rumors spread that the duel had been improperly carried out, that Broderick's pistol had been loaded with cotton wadding, and that Terry had actually killed him like a dog. Witnesses were found, and Terry was arrested. When the matter came to court, Terry declared that he wanted to be judged not in San Francisco but in the little town of San Antonio, because the court in San Francisco might be prejudiced. The law was on Terry's side, and the trial was moved to San Antonio. A jury was selected and a day set for the trial. Witnesses were to come from San Francisco to testify against Terry. The court was to open for business at 10:00 AM. The witnesses actually did gather on time for the ship, and left for San Antonio. But the ship's captain had been bribed, as well as the judge and the jury, so the witnesses did not reach San Antonio until 11:00, and the court had begun promptly at 10:00. Since there were no witnesses, the jury declared Terry not guilty, and he was released. When the ship arrived, the matter was over, and the witnesses came just in time to see Terry celebrate his freedom. This happened some time before our arrival. These are just some small examples of California happenings for you.

Now I will tell you how we spend our time. First of all, nearly all the respectable first class passengers who were with us on the *Washington* have paid visits to us; we occasionally meet with them now, and they try to help us in every possible way, although this kind of thoughtfulness is generally not customary among Americans. We have also become acquainted with a man named [J.] Mora Moss, who is president of a local ice company and director of several other companies. He is an elderly man, but very kind, and last Thursday he was our host at an excellent dinner. The only other person there was Senator [William M.] Gwin, who is a friend of our minister, Stoeckl. We sat down at the table at 6:00 PM and withdrew at 10:00 and returned home at 11:30. We have also been entertained by a man named Baum, who speaks Russian as well as if he had never left Russia. He is a director of one of the local companies. An elderly man, Gr., our acquaintance from Liverpool, has also entertained us. We have had to reciprocate all of these entertainments, and it is not inexpensive in a country where everything is counted in dollars, and a dollar is not considered much money. But it is necessary for us to get close to people who can give us interesting information about our colonies, both for the present and for the future, in relation to the development of trade and various enterprises. Without such information from persons who are experienced and acquainted with such matters, we would not be in a position to present a full report and our own opinions, and consequently we could not fulfill the wishes of the government.

It is customary here that every meeting and every business occasion be accompanied by some sort of hospitality. Without this we could not get anywhere. At home such expenditures would not be acceptable, but they are quite necessary other places, especially here in America; and they are not inconsiderable. But, God willing, we will somehow juggle things around, and provided everything goes well, hope that we will accomplish something really useful for the region. One can learn a great deal, using intelligent judgment, even from a minute undertaking. *It is only important not to dream, as our Company has been dreaming; not to order cigars, for example, to be sent from Manilla to Hamburg in order to send them on to the colonies, when one can ship anything one needs to Sitka via San Francisco, and it will be better quality and cost only half as much.*

We were also very pleased to meet Senator Gwin. Our envoy had given us a letter to him, and Gwin talked in great detail with us about the proposition he had submitted to the government in Washington about uniting Russia and America by means of an electric telegraph, and about organizing a Russian American Navigation Company which would operate between China, Japan and America in the Pacific. If he is re-elected to office he intends to work for these proposals. Unfortunately it is uncertain whether he will be re-elected. I also met Mr. [Perry McDonough] Collins, who was in St. Petersburg, traveled from there to Irkutsk, sailed down the Amur to Nikolaevsk, and has just recently returned to San Francisco. He has published a description of this journey which he made in 1856, and he kindly gave me a copy of it.*

25 October/6 November 1860

Today is the end of the local elections. Ever since morning special boxes have been set up at various corners where voters can put their ballots. These elections are held every four years. They are voting for the President of the Union, representatives or deputies, senators, and all the principal officials. On November 6 voters in all the states of the Union put their ballots in boxes such as these. Then a public announcement is made as to how many votes each candidate has received. This information is published in the newspapers. Every state sends the results of its elections to Washington, where the final count is made of the elections in all the various states, and the persons who receive the majority of votes are considered to have been elected to carry on the affairs of the states. In December they officially announce the names of persons who have been elected, and on March 4 the new officeholders enter the administration, and the old ones retire.

It is impossible to conceive how much intrigue, conniving and effort each party employs in order to win. There are processions, demonstrations, meetings and articles written. Some want the states to remain in their present condition. Others demand progress. Northern states demand that negroes be freed. On the

*Perry McDonough Collins. *Siberian Journey: Down the Amur to the Pacific,1856-1857*. Ed. Charles Vevier. (Madison, 1962)—Eds.

other hand, the southern states wish to keep slavery, and threaten to secede from the union if the government decides to free the negroes. Many think that sooner or later this is just what is going to happen. The southern states use the labor of negro slaves to operate enormous plantations which produce cotton and other raw materials; they will always find a market for this produce. The northern states, on the other hand, do not have raw materials, and their machines will grind to a halt. The divisiveness among the states will severely weaken the union, which will probably break up into several republics. At least, California raves on about separating and organizing its own republic.

Today we went to watch the voters casting their ballots. It is amazing how completely orderly everything was. There was no shouting or quarreling, whereas in former years there were often disputes involving revolvers. They anticipate, however, that in the evening when the elections are over, there will be celebrations in the streets, accompanied by fireworks and popguns, and many people will return home with broken noses.

On my free evenings I sometimes go to the local Italian opera. The orchestra consists of twelve musicians; there is a nine-man male choir, and a women's choir of six. The primadonna, Madame Escott, is fairly good, as is the tenor. The rest are very bad, and the bass is absolutely terrible; but since this is the best available, people listen. So I have had an opportunity to hear *Maritano* (Don Basile de Bozan), *Ernani*, *Trovatore* and *Lurline*; the latter, like *Maritano*, is performed in English. The theater is small and cannot boast of fancy decor.

26 October/7 November 1860

There is no way to find consecutive bits of free time; there is always one thing or another, and it is all part of our business. The ship *Tsaritsa* is finally going to be ready on Friday, October 28, and we will start our voyage on Saturday.

CIVIL AND SAVAGE ENCOUNTERS

I am very sad, my dear ones, not to have received your letters, all the more so since now God only knows when your letters will reach me. *The fact is that our [Russian] American Company does not have regular intercourse with its colonies. This is wild but true.* It is possible to communicate through Siberia in the summer months, although rarely; but from September to June all communication is discontinued because of the freeze. *However, sailing between Sitka and San Francisco is open the year around, and furthermore, there are English colonies between the two that have regular communication with San Francisco. It should be possible to find a hundred means to establish proper communications, and it would be desirable to do this, especially since the Governing Board is located 20,000 versts away. But apparently the Company is not doing anything about this. Every month it sends its correspondence from St. Petersburg to Hamburg, and no one worries about how long it will take to reach Sitka.*

As a result, this is what happens: Letters which are sent from St. Petersburg reach San Francisco in two months or so, and they are kept there until a ship arrives from Sitka with a cargo of ice. *Consequently, the order to the Chief Administrator of the colonies, instructing him to send a ship for us to California in October, which was sent from St. Petersburg in June, is still here, and only now is being forwarded to the colonies together with us.*

Consequently all dispatches, letters, et cetera which are received here after our departure will remain in San Francisco until another ship comes down from Sitka, and this will not be before the end of January or the beginning of February, because the lakes on Kodiak begin to freeze in December, at which time one has to wait for the ice to attain the requisite thickness, then cut it, load it on the ship, and send it to San Francisco. If that ship has good sailing weather and reaches San Francisco in two weeks, and everything goes smoothly on the return voyage and it manages to unload the ice and take on a new cargo, then it will take at least six weeks before it is back in Sitka. Thus any correspondence which arrives here in early November, our style, will not reach Sitka until late March or early April.

Don't be surprised if you do not have any more word from me after you receive this letter. Our letters will go from Sitka to California at the end of January or early in February, and so they will not reach St. Petersburg before March or April. The farther away we go, the more our letters will accumulate for the return voyage. So for now we will be patient and trust in God's mercy.

I had already folded the letter when the consul came in and told me there was still time to send it by post. I will take advantage of this to tell you a little about the climate here. There is no winter here. The thermometer in the severest period barely reaches freezing. In summer it is quite hot, but the main streets are laid out in such a manner that the sea breeze blows freely through them, which constantly raises dust. But nonetheless it is beautiful in spring and fall! The grass and vegetation die in summer because of the heat, but after several rainy days in fall there is a second spring, when the grass turns green again and the vegetation comes back to life and flowers blossom with new beauty. At this very moment there is a gorgeous bouquet in front of me, with exquisite roses, lilies, cyclamen, all picked from our consul's little garden. There are roses of every hue—crimson, red, white and yellow. The weather is perfect, almost no wind, and both day and night I walk about in a single coat, with no scarf or other wrap. It is too bad that Sitka does not have weather such as this. When we get there it will be rainy and foggy . . .

Paul.

San Francisco   2/14 November 1860

In my last letter to you, my bonne Maman and chère Soeur P., I informed you that we were leaving San Francisco on Saturday, 29 October, our style. In fact, by 8:00 AM we were aboard our ship, but a heavy fog, which lasted all during low tide, which is the time that would have been favorable for our departure, forced us to stand at anchor. On Sunday there was such a strong headwind that the steamer did not dare to tow us out from the bay. Having thus lost two days, we decided to stay here until the arrival of a steamer from Panama, which should bring the mail. We made our decision on the strength of the fact that two or three days will make no difference, but if we left without waiting for the mail, then our papers and letters would not reach us in Sitka until January. We decided to wait for the mail, and so as not to be a burden on our consul, we rented a furnished room for $2.00 each.

Today at 8:00 AM the Panamanian ship finally arrived, and I received your letters of 6 September. This is very rapid, if one considers the distance between us. Do not worry about me. When you were cold and wet from the rain in St. Petersburg, we were languishing from the heat, and for us the rain was a decided blessing. From here we will be sailing on a good ship which has made a circumnavigation of the world. The captain is an experienced man and is very familiar with the sailing to Sitka, and he keeps his ship in good order. Our quarters are ample and good, we have plenty of provisions, and this will not be the first time I have encountered a strong wind. I learned about the wreck of the *Plastun* from the American newspapers, but they never mentioned the name of the ship. I am glad for my friend, Mtskv., who was commanding officer of the *Plastun*, but had to relinquish the ship to another officer because of illness. I saw Mtskv. in St. Petersburg before I left; he had just arrived via Panama.

Thanks to several friends here, we have never been bored. In the mornings we have been occupied with business, gathering the necessary information we needed, and in the evenings on our free days we have visited several acquaintances, or have gone to the theater. The weather throughout this entire period has been beautiful, very warm, so that only occasionally did I wear a light coat in the evenings to keep from catching cold from the dampness. My health is generally very good, so I can't ask for more than that. If it continues, then with God's help I hope I will have enough strength to carry out this mission, which is going to be very difficult, judging by what we already know at this point. But God is merciful.

I believe I will return home through Europe. I even think my companion will also go by this route, although the sea voyage has caused him great discomfort. But there appear to be circumstances which dictate our need to return to Washington, especially since the change in the American government. Of all the parties, the Republicans have the upper hand, and they are anticipating great changes in politics. The southern states wish to secede in case negroes are to be freed. California dreams only about how to organize itself into a separate republic. In one word, only God knows how all of this will end. Meanwhile, there is some talk about constructing a telegraph line through our colonies and through Siberia to Europe, as well as about setting up communication by ship between China, Japan, the Amur and San Francisco. In short, the Americans are *thinking* about establishing close ties with Russia, which would be very good both for Siberia and for our colonies.

Yesterday I went to the opera to hear a performance of *Martha*, and although there were flaws in the primadonna's voice, the opera was not bad.

I will send my next letter from Sitka on the first ship that leaves from there . . .

Sitka [Island], New Arkhangel   27 November/9 December 1860

I am starting this letter to you, my chère Maman and Soeur, immediately upon my arrival on Sitka. After I responded to your letters, which I received in San Francisco, we went out that evening to hear *Norma*, and at 11:00 AM on the 3/15 November we finally boarded the *Tsaritsa*. When the afternoon tide began to go out the ship was towed by a tug, and we were at sea by about 3:00 PM. Shortly after that we had quite a strong headwind. Of course

Kostlivtsov immediately became seasick and went to the cabin, so I did some reading.

We were usually joined by Captain Riddell, commanding officer of *Tsaritsa*, for breakfast, lunch and evening tea. Riddell was always accompanied by a large black dog named Castor, whose head had been split open in San Francisco, but thanks to Riddell's constant attention the wound healed and he is now completely restored to health. Three seamen and the captain's son, a lad of 17, have a separate table.

A strong headwind blew for two days, then there was a dead calm with a tremendous swell which lasted until 12/24 November. After we had been at sea for two days one of our sailors died, apparently from pneumonia. *The Company does not provide either a doctor or a feldsher on its ships*, and since neither the captain nor the navigator had any knowledge of how to treat this illness, although they are good naval specialists, the poor sailor, lacking adequate treatment, departed from this world to the next, *where he will probably be better off than in the service of the Russian American Company*. His Finnish fellow-countrymen said a prayer over the departed, and lowered the body over the side. This took place at 3:00 PM on 9/21 November.

On November 12/24 we encountered a fair wind in 39° latitude; on 13/25 this turned into a storm. This storm raged fiercely right up until we reached Sitka; one day we had to reef almost all our sails, but the next day there was a dead calm with huge swells. The storms were accompanied by fierce gusts of wind with a downpour of rain and hail. Our vessel was tossed about like a nutshell, but thanks to the strength of the mast and the spars, we lost only two sails which were torn by the wind. It was difficult to concentrate on anything in the cabin, so I either read or went up on deck to amuse myself with Castor and two kittens. We were fed as God provided; although we carried fresh provisions, the ship rolled so much and the cook was so inexperienced that we usually had to make do with cabbage soup and a bit of fried meat, although apples and grapes were consumed in rather large quantities.

At last we came in sight of Sitka Bay on the morning of 20 November/2 December, but the wind was so strong we had to reef all the upper sails and put back out to sea. For three days we held off near Sitka, but could not make an observation, nor could we survey the shore because of the dense fog. At last on 24 November/6 December everything became calmer, the weather cleared a little, and the coastline was visible; but because of the headwind we could not tack into the bay until night. We thought the wind would come up again at night, and send us back out to sea, but fortunately there was just one strong squall, and at last, at 4:00 AM on 25 November/7 December, in total darkness, we managed to enter the bay and fired off a cannon to announce our arrival. At 11:00 a tug came out, and at noon the tug *Nikolai* towed us into New Arkhangel, where we anchored 100 sazhens from shore.

The Chief Administrator, Captain [Johan Hampus] Furuhjelm [Chief Administrator, 1859-64], immediately came to meet us, and we went ashore with him. We gave the members of the crew a silver ruble each, and thanked the captain and officers for the successful sailing to Stika. And so here I am on Sitka! Do you want to know what it is like? Well, listen.

In 57° northern latitude, not far from the mainland of North America, there is a continuation of the Russian possessions, and here is a small island which has been given the name of Sitka. On the western shore of this island, in the depth of a quiet bay which is protected by numerous rocky little islands, the settlement of New Arkhangel is located, capital of our North American colonies. As one approaches Sitka from the sea one sees ranks of high mountains which are steep and covered with dense vegetation. The sea reaches right up to the base of these mountains, and at high tide runs up to the homes in the settlement which are spread along the shore for a distance of about one verst. The small rocky islands are forested for the most part, and are grouped in front of the settlement, so they create a peaceful harbor where ships are quite protected from the choppy seas which rage against the hills of the bay during a northwest wind.

The dwelling of the Chief Administrator, or the "fort" as it is called, stands on a high rocky cape which protrudes into the sea. The building is a large, ugly two-story wooden structure with many annexes. The whole is painted yellow, and is surrounded by a wooden wall in which there are cannon embrasures and gun batteries. One enters this fort with the aid of wooden steps. The Chief Administrator lives here, and the ammunition depot is here, and in case of attack by the Indians, or *Kolosh* [Tlingits] as they are known here, the inhabitants of the settlement may run here under the protection of the guns. At the base of the cliff on which the fortress stands, along the shore, there are the harbor facilities, warehouses, et cetera. Then to one side there is the settlement, which consists of small wooden houses where service personnel and Company officials, prikaschiks and lower ranks live. Farther on there is a wooden cathedral, the club, the Bishop's residence, and the infirmary. The street, the only one in the settlement, is narrow; since it rains all the time it is quite impassable because of the mud for at least three-quarters of the year. Consequently boards have been laid all along the middle of the street. On the other side of the fort, partway up the hill, there are some workshops; beyond them there is a wooden wall which separates the Russian settlement from the Kolosh. At one place the Kolosh settlement comes almost up to the wall, and continues along the shore. A wooden fortification has been built near the sea where the wall starts. Its ordnance is aimed at the Kolosh settlement. Alongside the batteries there is a market where trade goes on with the Kolosh every day. (I will tell you later about this market and about trade.) Farther on up the hill near the wall, there is a small church for the baptized Kolosh, but services are rarely held there because the Kolosh simply do not attend. Many of them have been baptized, thanks to gifts and entertainment, but they do not like to go to church without being rewarded in some way. If someone were to announce that they would receive a cup of vodka after each service they attended, then of course the church would always be full to overflowing; but without this, they do not go to pray.

From this brief description you can grasp some small understanding of New Arkhangel. When we went ashore, we went with

Furuhjelm to the home of the Chief Administrator. The main rooms on the upper floor are usually empty, and they had been set aside for our living quarters. I have been given a large room with two windows which look out onto a little creek, and beyond that to the settlement; there are three other windows from which I can see the workshops, the wall, the Kolosh church and *sorabor*, or settlement. Beyond these, the harbor. The view is quite good. The room is warm and comfortable. There is a billiards room next door, and on the other side, a large reception room where certain of the service personnel, officers and officials often come to dine with the Chief Administrator. Beyond the reception room is our own sitting room and my companion's room.

The first day we were quite content to have a walk along the settlement and in the evening to have a bath in the Russian bathhouse. The following day at 11:00 AM we visited the local Bishop, and found him saying Mass in his home chapel, for it was a Saint's Day (St. Innokentii). After Mass we served at public prayer and then had breakfast with the Bishop, Father Peter. He is quite well educated and is said to be highly regarded here. Later we paid a few more visits and returned home for dinner; we stayed home in the evening. Yesterday, Sunday, we went to the Cathedral at 9:30 for the service, and after that all the local service personnel came to meet us, and the Bishop also paid us a visit.

The introductions did not take place without some laughter. There were some persons whom they had forgotten to inform, and there they were, appearing before Furhjelm with petitions saying that they had served the Company for 15 years and were being deprived of the honor of being introduced. Of course Furuhjelm pacified them by saying that this was an oversight, and introduced them to us along with the others. Then a *toion*, or elder, appeared before us. A toion is a person who has been appointed over the Kolosh by the Russian administration.

This toion wore a ceremonial caftan or robe. His name is Mikhailo; he is a baptized Indian. He does not speak Russian, but is completely loyal to us. He was fully aware of his position, and presented himself to us in full magnificence. He was clothed in a

CIVIL AND SAVAGE ENCOUNTERS

brocaded cloak with silver tassels and lace, a raspberry-colored silk sash with gold fringe which cinched his belly, above the sash a naval sabre on a black thong, and in his hands he held a small triangular hat such as Frederick the Great used to wear, but with a tall plume of white, blue, rose, yellow and black feathers. It is impossible to imagine anything more hilarious than this figure. He entered very gravely, held out his hand to us, and from his inside pocket he took a certificate which had been given to him by the Russian government testifying to the fact that he had been named a toion. Through an interpreter we told him that he and all the rest of the elders and Indians could appear before us if they had any business to discuss with us. He replied that he was vey glad that we had come, and that he would transmit our words to the Indians, and they would then think about what they wished to request of us, since there is no need to disturb important persons with silly speeches. Then he very gravely took his leave, shook our hands, and with measured steps he left the room.

In the evening there was a meeting for men in the club, and we went there to have a look at the local club. Meetings usually begin at 5:00 PM and end at 11:00. The club consists of two rooms, a billiards room and a salon. The salon is not very large, it has an unpainted floor, and this is where they dance to the music of the fortepiano when they hold a ball. They have what they call family evenings, when the ladies come and bring their work with them; at such times the men do not drink at all. Anyone who is thirsty must be satisfied with tea and water. Since the club is not at all wealthy, each membership is quite important, so we signed up as annual members and paid our dues of 25 paper rubles each.

Incidentally, everything here is counted in paper rubles. There is absolutely no money in circulation, neither hard cash nor bills of credit; rather, they use colonial marks similar to those used in Reval [present Tallinn, Estonia]; they are in denominations of 10, 25 and 50 kopecks, and 1, 5 and 10 paper rubles. These marks are distributed from the administrative office and are used to purchase everything the Company has for sale in the warehouse, since no outsider can bring anything in to the colonies to sell. These same marks are also given as pay to the Kolosh, and in exchange the Indians can buy whatever they need from the warehouses. *This is very profitable for the Company: it pays for all labor with marks, and receives them back for goods, on which of course it has added a certain markup, so that in actuality the Company pays nothing for labor.*

Now a few words about the people who are subject to Russia, or who are considered to be subject. They are usually divided into two categories, the Aleuts and the Indians, and each of these is divided into many tribes. Aleuts are peaceful, quiet and lazy people. Sometimes they were subjugated willingly, but more often unwillingly; they work for the Company. They are all under the supervision of *prikaschiks* [agents] or *baidarshchiks* [overseers] and are kept busy hunting on the islands. For each pelt, they receive payment at a set rate. In its turn the Company, also at an agreed rate, provides them with all necessities, both for hunting and for living. For this purpose, on all the islands where Aleuts live, the Company has built small shops which are supplied from the main colonial warehouses. *Sometimes it happens that an Aleut asks for tea, but receives clothing; he may ask for red cloth and receive blue; he may request flour and be given footwear.* The tribe is generally weak and is gradually dying out. They are willingly baptized, and willingly go to church and fulfill their obligations. The offspring of Aleuts and Russians are called *creoles*. There are quite a few of these on Sitka. The children are educated in schools at Company expense and sing quite harmoniously in church but swear intolerably.

The Indians, of whom the closest neighbors to us are the Kolosh, are an entirely different matter. They are intelligent, warlike and savage; they have a deep aversion to civilization of any kind. They work willingly if they know that their work will be rewarded, but they also like to be lazy and to lie around in idleness. They are always armed with knives, and often have revolvers and guns which they get from the English and Americans. They are all very good shots and they are brave but they fear cannister shot and balls. Some of the previous Chief Administrators have been very

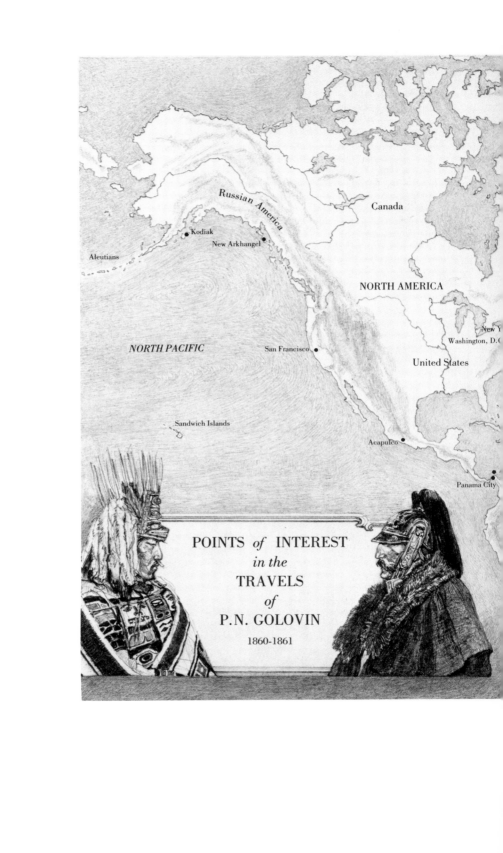

POINTS *of* INTEREST
in the
TRAVELS
of
P.N. GOLOVIN
1860-1861

GREENLAND

St Petersburg

Russia

Hamburg
Liverpool   Cologne   Berlin
London   Dresden
Dieppe   Frankfurt
          Brussels
     Paris

EUROPE

fax

NORTH ATLANTIC

AFRICA

UTH AMERICA

SOUTH ATLANTIC

Map by Karen Beyers

much afraid of them, which has given the Kolosh much confidence. More than once there has been fighting. There is no doubt that if firm measures had been taken they would long ago have been brought into complete obedience and would be in fear of God, but unfortunately all measures which have been undertaken up until now have been inadequate and indecisive. The result is that New Arkhangel is constantly in a state of siege.

The Kolosh are not allowed to enter the settlement, so trade takes place in the market in the following manner. A building has been constructed below the battery in which they put all the goods which the Kolosh generally need. Behind the building in the Kolosh settlement there is a small empty bit of land enclosed by a high palisade—this is the market. The Kolosh enter through a draw-wicket gate, which, if necessary, can be instantly let down. There is a window in the wall of the building or warehouse which is closed from inside with a heavy shutter. When the Kolosh come into the market in the morning and bring in their goods, consisting of wild goats (*iamans*), game, fish and potatoes, the window in this little shop is opened, and the Company prikashchik receives the goods from each Indian at a set price and gives him either marks or goods in return, also at a set rate. The Kolosh are not allowed to sell their goods to any foreigner living in New Arkhangel. When the trade with the Kolosh is ended, the inhabitants of New Arkhangel come to the shop and buy however much they need of iaman, potatoes and fish at the set rate, also paying in marks.

Because the Kolosh are so dangerous the Company has for some time been thinking of banishing them from the settlement altogether, but they are afraid that in that case there would be no fresh provisions in New Arkhangel, because *Russians do not go out to hunt in the forest, have very few gardens, and have no livestock except pigs. There are only five or six cows and four horses on the whole island.* Salted beef is brought in from Aian to provision service personnel and other inhabitants. They have not introduced livestock on the grounds that there is no hay, so it would have to be brought in from California. *But actually only the coastal areas have been explored on Sitka, Kodiak, and the other more important islands. No one has been into the interior of the islands, and people just say there cannot be anything of interest there.*

These are my first impressions of this land which is terra incognita for Russia and local inhabitants. I am beginning this letter today, and it will be sent in several days, along with some salted fish, to the Sandwich Islands; from there the letters will go to California, then to Russia via the usual route. When the ship has unloaded the fish it will sail to Russia around Cape Horn. We are thinking of sending back several items that seem to be superfluous. We brought so much with us from St. Petersburg that we really don't know what to do with it, and since it appears that we will return by the same route, we will not want to carry extra luggage with us and have to pay for it on ships and railroads. Just for example, for the trip across the Isthmus of Panama we had to pay $50 for our luggage, which is 62.50 silver rubles.

Sitka, New Arkhangel   1/12 December 1860

In order to familiarize oneself with the region, one has to read a great deal and ask many questions, and in this way one finds out much that is of no small interest, that is new, and at the same time is both amusing and original. The customs of the local savages, their way of life, their habits and traditions—all of this is an object for study. For example, here are some things I have learned from books and tales about the Kolosh. The Kolosh believe in the existence of a God who had no beginning and will have no end, whom they call El. They believe that before El there was permanent darkness on the earth. El lived in the forest and hunted. Once he killed a raven which was white because all ravens were white then. When he had skinned the raven, El garbed himself in the pelt and began to fly so high in the sky that he hit his nose against the clouds and was trapped there until with great effort he managed to free his nose. In this manner El frequently transformed himself into various creatures, but most often into the white raven.

El heard people complain that there was no light anywhere, and he wished to help them. He discovered that light was stored in three boxes hidden in the home of a rich toion. But so vigilantly did this toion guard the boxes that not even his only daughter, for whom he would do anything, was allowed to touch the boxes. El flew to the toion's home, transformed himself into a tiny bit of grass, and stuck to the lip of a cup from which the toion's daughter was drinking. She did not notice El, and swallowed him and became pregnant. Eight months later she gave birth to a son, who was El. Her father came to love his grandson very much, even more than he had earlier loved his daughter.

One time El was playing on his mother's lap, and he began to cry and scream, and refused to eat. He kept pointing at the boxes. At last the toion, in order to soothe the child, gave him one of the boxes, but warned his servant to make absolutely certain the child did not open the box. The infant calmed down, and as he played, he crawled toward the door of the *barabora*, and then crawled through the door outside, and as soon as he saw that the servant was paying no attention to him, he opened the box—and instantly stars spilled across the sky.

The toion became violently angry with the servant, but did not punish the child. A few days later El begged for another box in the same way, and again he went out the door of the barabora and opened the box—and the moon appeared in the sky. Finally he managed to get the third box, but the toion declared that if he opened that one, he would come to harm. El crawled out of the barabora, however, opened the box, and released the sun into the sky. Then he instantly transformed himself into the white raven and flew off.

Another time he realized the earth had not even a drop of fresh water, and found that all the water was being stored by a man named Kanuk, the founder of the Kolosh wolf tribe who lived on a small island not far from the eastern cape of Sitka. The water was stored in a well which Kanuk kept covered with a lid, and he would personally lie on top of the lid. El went to the island and became acquainted with Kanuk, who entertained him and then fell asleep on the well cover. Then El found some dog dung and put it under Kanuk. He awakened Kanuk and said: "Kanuk! Look what has happened to you! You must be sick!" Kanuk jumped up and thought this misadventure had happened while he was dreaming. He ran to the shore to wash. El, meanwhile, changed himself into the white raven, opened the lid of the well, drank, and carrying as much water in his mouth as he could, he flew out through the chimney. But at the top someone stopped him, and Kanuk started a fire in the stove and began to smoke El, who suffered terribly, but did not let the water drop from his mouth. He finally flew off, all black. From that time on, all ravens have been black. El flew over the earth, letting drops of fresh water fall on it, and wherever a small drop fell, little streams began to flow; where large drops fell, lakes and great rivers appeared.

In precisely this same way, in order to give people fire El transformed himself into the raven and stole a glowing ember from one island and brought it to land. The ember kept burning while he was flying, and burned half of El's nose, but he still managed to bring back a bit of glowing coal and dropped it down onto the earth. The coal hit a rock and a tree, and ever since then there is fire in the rocks and in the woods.

In addition to El, the Kolosh believe in spirits who, according to their view, are the souls of the dead. Generally, however, they believe that souls do not die, but are in a special place, and that some come back to earth in the form of spirits, and others are again transformed into persons. Thus, when a rich toion dies, they try to send servants with him to the other world. For that purpose they select a *kalga*, or slave, belonging to the toion, and kill him. He definitely must die the same way the toion did. If the toion was shot, then the kalga is shot. If the toion drowned, the kalga drowns. If the toion died from some illness, then the kalga is placed into the ground face upward, and they put a stick across his neck, and the relatives of the deceased sit on both ends of the stick and stay there until the kalga has been strangled. Our administration has now declared to the Kolosh that they must not do such things, so now instead of killing slaves they sell them to the

CIVIL AND SAVAGE ENCOUNTERS

Russians. But this is done only on Sitka, under our cannon. In other places they still kill and strangle slaves, just as before.

The Kolosh are not usually violent, and rarely attack unless they are drunk; but they are irritable and vindictive in the extreme. An insulted Kolosh is not satisfied until he either stabs the person who insulted him, or shoots him. A blood feud is handed down from generation to generation. A long time ago a group of Stikine Kolosh killed 70 Sitka Kolosh. The Sitka took vengeance in blood for blood, and over a course of several years they managed to kill 30 men, leaving 40 to be avenged. Then it seemed that they were somewhat reconciled, that the Sitka Kolosh appeared to have renounced the feud, and they began to trade with the Stikine again. Then once when 40 Stikine men came to Sitka, the Sitka Kolosh invited them into a barabora to carouse, and they immediately killed every one of them.

Chastity is not one of the virtues of the Kolosh. Kolosh creoles are definitely much better looking than Aleut creoles. The former have quite regular features and large eyes; the latter have Mongol features, with flat noses and narrow eyes, just like the Kalmyks.

5/17 December 1860

Well, we have already been on Sitka for 10 days. I cannot say that time has gone slowly, but the monotony is dreadful. After dinner we generally stroll along the street, and then along the shore to the so-called Rock, which is a quarter of a verst from the settlement, and then we go back home. There is no other place to walk here. Yesterday, however, there was a little diversion. Behind the settlement there is a small lake which has already frozen over, and the ice is quite thick. Yesterday, Sunday, the young people here went to the lake to go ice-skating. A few ladies came, too; they are usually pushed around the lake on chairs on runners.

A great many Kolosh, both men and women, also came to the lake. Many of them had painted their faces for the holiday.

Imagine a woman whose whole face is heavily painted with a black pigment, while her eyebrows are painted bright red. There are several hoops of silver and copper, and tiny shells in her ear lobes. Her nose is pierced through the center, and there is a silver hoop and a silver or perhaps a thick wooden labret inserted in an opening made a little below the lower lip. The thicker this wooden insert is, the more distinguished the tribe to which the woman belongs. Nearly all of them, with very few exceptions, walk barefoot and do not feel the cold. Their entire costume consists of a shirt, over which they wear a wool blanket in black or red. The men drape themselves quite nicely in these blankets, which the toions decorate with silver paillettes. Some of the men do not paint their faces black, but instead, decorate them with various designs in red, blue or black. There were some of the Kolosh women who did not paint their faces, and we noticed several who were quite good looking. All of the women were squatting on the ice, wrapped up in their blankets, and they peered at us, all the while chewing tobacco. *I am certain that if reasonable means were used, the Kolosh could easily become accustomed to our ways, especially since they do not move about from one place to another, but lead a settled way of life, like to work, and are already putting up fences.* In our presence one Kolosh went up to Furuhjelm and asked to be hired as a sailor on a ship that is sailing to Kronshtadt.

This ship will leave here on the 8th or 10th of December, and I will send this letter aboard her to the Sandwich Islands. By my calculations I think that you will receive it by the middle or end of April, or possibly in the early part of May. Everything will depend on when the ship leaves for the Sandwich Islands. In January another ship is sailing directly to California, and I will also send you a letter aboard that one, and it may well happen that you will receive both letters at the same time. Since we plan to leave here in April to inspect the colonies, and will not be returning to Sitka, when we have concluded our inspection we will sail directly to California. When you receive this letter, write to me in New York. After that we still do not know which route we will take from New York, but probably we will travel via Vienna and Warsaw.

Yesterday was St. Nicholas' Day, and there was a service in the Cathedral. When they sang "Mnogie leta,"* the cannon began to fire a salute. After that we paid a visit to the Bishop, and then there was an official dinner at the Furuhjelms'. At 6:30 PM, by the light of little lamps, we set out for the club. Everyone had already gathered there. There was an orchestra of four volunteer musicians—two violins, a cello and a flute; the pianist was ill and unable to play. Upon our entrance they struck up some Polish music, and we promenaded with the more distinguished local ladies. There were quite a few people there. Among the ladies were the wives of officers serving in the Company: captains, *chinovniks* and prikashchiks. The midwife and the deaconess were also there. Among the creole women there were some extremely amusing examples. Some of the young girls were not bad: there was one young creole girl who is going to marry the supervisor of the local school; there was also a young Swedish girl; but all the others were far from attractive. There was also the daughter of a prikashchik, a plain girl of about 20. The Bishop's secretary has proposed to her; he is greatly attracted by her dowry, which amounts to 1,000 rubles, both paper and silver. No one knows what the service will be like; the family is keeping it a secret; but the dowry is alluring to the young man who seeks the hand of that young girl.

Everyone had a good time and danced until all were exhausted. At 11:30 PM we sat down to have supper. They drank to our health, and we drank to the health of the Chief Administrator and of the ladies. Finally at 12:30 we went home, leaving the rest freee to enjoy themselves. We returned home by the light of blue flares which had been lighted along the road from the club to the home of the Chief Administrator. The cold here is quite severe, but the sea never freezes. In general the weather has been beautiful. I hope that by January the ice on

---

*"Many years. . . ," a song customarily sung on birthdays and feast days.—Eds.

the lake will reach the required thickness so that it will be possible to send a load of ice to San Francisco; that way we will receive news from you.

New Arkhangel   17/29 December 1860

A week ago a Company ship, *Imperator Nikolai*, left here, and with it I sent a letter to you, my dear Maman and Soeur P. The ship is on its way to Kronshtadt, and is going around the Horn; it must stop at the Sandwich Islands. There it will transmit our letters to the agent of the Company, who will send them to California. From there they will go by the usual route through Panama to Europe. Assuming that *Nikolai* reaches the Sandwich Islands in 20 days, and that the journey from there to Petersburg will take about two months, I calculate that my letter will not reach you before March 20. Probably another ship will leave from here with a cargo of ice for California some time before the holiday, and I will send this second letter to you aboard her. I do not look for news from you before mid-March, which is the time at which the ship from California is due to return. Then I will not hear anything at all from you until June, because we are going to inspect the colonies in April, and then we will go directly to San Francisco, where all of your letters and dispatches will be awaiting us.

Well, we have been on Sitka three weeks already! It is a good thing that there is plenty of work to do, because otherwise the boredom might make me think about the water, since the sea is right under our windows. Because we have dinner so early the day drags on forever. You write, you read, you listen, you ask questions. In the morning you go to the shops, the battery, and various harbor installations. After dinner you walk to the end of the settlement or to the Rock. Half an hour later you return home, and then back to the books, back to the letters.

And so, day after day, today is the same as yesterday.
From books to pen, and from pen to books . . .

The present Chief Administrator, Furuhjelm, is doing everything he can to keep us from being bored, but the means to avoid boredom are inadequate. My main problem is that I do not have any news from either of you, and I don't know anything of what is happening in the rest of the world. It is terrible how this affects one's spirits. One good thing is that the weather has been clear ever since we arrived here. One looks out onto the peaceful sea and the bright sunshine, and somehow the spirit is rekindled. But this joy will probably not continue. They say that such constant good weather is very unusual here. Soon the rains will begin and continue for several weeks on end. There will be winds so strong that you can only go about on the street by crawling on all fours, and that only under the cover of the houses. That will be a delight! I must confess that when all of this is over and we leave here, both sound and healthy, I will be ecstatic to meet even Americans. And there are people who have spent their whole lives here, who have grown old and will die here on Sitka!

A few days ago we paid a visit to some local people, and on the way visited two old bachelor prikashchiks who live together in a small room in the club. They left Russia together in 1823. One of them, [N.V.] Alekseev, spent 18 years on the island of Unalaska, which has no trees and is populated only by Aleuts. The other, Uglichaninov, spent most of his time on the island of Kodiak. Several years ago they were reunited on Sitka, where they both served as senior prikashchiks in the warehouse. Every day from 8:00 AM until 7:00 PM they can be found in the warehouse, where they either hand out or take in goods. And so go their lives. Both of them are cheerful, ruddy little old men, much beloved by everyone, and are altogether satisfied with their lot. Alekseev has told us a great deal about hunting and about the life of the Aleuts. He speaks of his life on Unalaska with tender emotion, and he speaks warmly of the Aleuts; he is ecstatic when he tells about the hunting trips he went on after sea otters. "You won't believe," he says enthusiastically, "that on those hunting expeditions there is a kind of martial atmosphere. Around 150 baidarkas go out, with two Aleuts in each, wearing hats decorated with sea lion whiskers, carrying arrows and spears—and I love to watch them. Many times I went out to hunt with them, just out of curiosity." I like these old men very much. They remind me a little of the old world *pomeshchiks* [landed gentry]. I am certain that if anything happened to Uglichaninov, then Alekseev would not survive him by more than a few days. These are truly contented men.

And here we are, bored because we don't see anything, and during our walks we find our only pleasure in watching for a few minutes how the ravens on the shore tear a sea creature apart, how a pig chases a dog which is barking at little piglets, or how a billygoat tears the bark off a big shrub.

This sea creature resembles a black cuttlefish and is disgusting in appearance. Imagine a round, jelly-like mass, of a reddish color, about half an *arshin* in diameter, armed with six jelly-like legs which are each about one-and-a-half arshins long. The entire upper portion of each leg, from the trunk of the body to the tip, is dotted with a row of little whitish discs which are hollow inside. The creature expels the air from these, and then when it extends its tentacles and touches some object or other, these discs adhere so firmly to the object that it is impossible to pull them off. It is the same kind of process as a cupping glass. Sometimes it happens that it fastens one of its tentacles onto the leg of a Kolosh who is bathing. Then the only thing to do is to cut off the tentacle from the creature; only then, with great effort, can one detach it from the person's leg. The local Kolosh and creoles are very fond of eating these creatures. They beat the meat with a pounder and cook it in salt water. They say that the meat is very tender and compares very favorably with the meat of shellfish but is more flavorful. They brought a live specimen to show us, and Furuhjelm ordered it to be served with mayonnaise, but I firmly declined; after seeing this creature crawling around our entrance hall, I was persuaded that not even the tiniest bite of it, no matter how temptingly prepared, would go down my throat.

To put it in a nutshell, there is not much variety in our food here. There is very little livestock in the colonies because it would take many persons to tend them, and everyone is busy hunting.

Consequently there is no fresh beef. Salted beef is brought in from Aian, of quite poor quality. It is made from animals that have been driven down from Iakutsk. If you will look at the map you will see what distances these wretched creatures must cover before reaching Sitka in the form of salted meat. The Kolosh bring iaman to the market, and halibut, and game birds that look like our black cock, and partridge. There are quite a few pigs. So for dinner we may have a purée of halibut or iaman bouillon; then halibut or iaman with sauce; then boiled iaman, or from time to time, the black cock bird. I am certain that both the iaman and the halibut will make my stomach turn for many years to come. And in St. Petersburg wild goat is a delicacy! *However, it is thanks to the good will of the Kolosh that we have this food. If they suddenly decided to become angry, which has happened during the year, they would stop bringing meat and produce to the market and the whole colony would go hungry and would be forced to feed itself on Aian salted beef and on salted fish*. This would be no problem for the creoles, because they eat dried salmon (*iukola*) with pleasure, accompanied by sea lion or whale blubber. But the Russian nature is not strengthened by such fare. The very smell of iukola makes me retch, although in my time I have smelled a fair amount of every sort of rot. For this reason we court the Kolosh in order to propitiate them, at least for the period of our stay here.

Several days ago we were informed that the Kolosh toions wanted to see us. We set a day, and last Wednesday, 14 December, at 11:00 AM, about 30 toions appeared in the club. A row of chairs had been set up for them in the room, and against the opposite wall there were three velvet chairs for Kostlivtsov, Furuhjelm and me. This time the Kolosh wore their ceremonial costumes. The Russian toion Mikhailo wore a fleet skipper's coat; three Kolosh hostages wore blue dress coats and trousers with red stripes down the sides; the rest of the toions slipped on ceremonial costumes over their shirts. The costumes were blue, faced in red, with little silver decorations which look rather like hammered silver lace. The costume was completed with boots and shoes—a luxury which the Kolosh allow themselves only on special occasions. The Kolosh do not wear headcovering as they are warm enough in their long, thick tarlike black hair. They all sat silent, awaiting our entrance, with their elbows on their knees and their chins in their hands. Some were very picturesque in their costume, and deftly draped themselves in their blankets. Bronze faces, black eyes shining like coal, broad shoulders, muscular limbs— all of this indicated energy and strength. We entered and sat in the chairs. The toions raised their heads but did not rise, as this is not their custom. They were informed through an interpreter that in accordance with their wishes we had come to converse with them, and that if they had anything to say to us they could say it; however, they must not all speak at once, but rather, one at a time, and that we would listen. Without changing their pose, the toions nodded.

The silence continued for several minutes, for each considered it unseemly to begin speaking too soon. Finally one old toion raised his head and folded his arms, and with fitting emphasis and intonation made the following speech.

> Russians and baptized Kolosh believe in God and Jesus Christ who are in heaven. When the weather is bad for a long time they pray and ask God to give them good weather. Sometimes they pray for one, two, three days. Finally God listens to their prayer and sends them good weather. We are not baptized but we also believe in God who is in heaven. We prayed to God, not one day, not two days, but several days, and God listened to our prayer and allowed us to see you; and so for us the sun rose and the good weather came, because if we cannot see the sovereign Emperor himself, who is strong and powerful, then we do see you, whom the sovereign Emperor sent to see us and converse with us. So we rejoice and praise God. I have spoken.

The rest of the toions silently nodded their heads as a sign of agreement, and several approvingly smacked their lips.

We remained silent for a little time, then replied that we were also glad to see them. We informed them that the sovereign looks after the Russians and the Kolosh equally and considers them all his children, and makes no distinction between them, and that he has sent us here to see what his Kolosh children are doing. We said we were pleased to hear from the Chief Administrator that at present they are living peacefully and quietly and do not quarel or brawl. This is how it must continue to be, and in the future they must come closer to the Russians and be friends. We said the Chief Administrator will always protect each of them and fulfill their just requests, if they make such requests humbly, and not grab their weapons and shout and make threats. Good men will always be well treated. But if they start to be rowdy and hostile, and take up weapons, then the hostages will be the first to pay with their heads, and the others will be punished without mercy. They must take this warning once and for all, and keep their subjects from disorderly conduct and violence.

Again there was several minutes of silence, and again one of the toions responded. "There was a time when the Russians who settled on our land treated us badly, shed our blood, and we avenged blood with blood as it is our custom to do, handed down from our fathers. But then the Russians became friendly toward us, and we became friendly toward the Russians, and now we live in peace. Sometimes there are arguments, when liquor makes hotheads who become angry and quarrelsome, but then they become peaceful again and everything is fine. If we are insulted we petition, but we do not personally take vengeance for insult, and we live in peace and will continue to live in peace, because this is good." Then several of the toions gave us written certificates issued to them by Chief Administrators, attesting to their loyalty to the Russians, and stating that they had performed various services. The Kolosh treasure such certificates very much, and hand them down from father to son. We informed them that we had authorized the Chief Administrator to issue holiday rewards to everyone who has such a certificate, and the rest must strive to merit such certificates. Then we said farewell and gave orders that each one be given tea, a little cup of vodka, and dinner in the home of the Russian toion, Mikhailo. In order to extend our hospitality to them, they were given two *charkas* of rum each, rice porridge with syrup (this is their favorite treat) and tea.

The Kolosh went away very much pleased, and made merry in Mikhailo's quarters until 2:00 AM. Mikhailo did not lose by this celebration, however, because in the course of treating his guests he also drank a great deal. Then when they got around to singing, it seemed to him that the little son of one of the toions was not playing well on the drum, so he took away the drumstick and as he tried to show him how it should be done, he accidentally hit the child on the head with the drumstick hard enough that his forehead started to bleed. In order to forego the vengeance of blood for blood, the next day he had to pay the boy's father 30 paper rubles. Then when the carousing guests left, they took his plates away so they could feed porridge to their children and wives at home, and of course they did not return the plates. You may be certain that we compensated Mikhailo for his losses, but warned him to stay sober.

The Kolosh language is not sonorous. One constantly hears the sound "kkh" which is pronounced through the nose while breathing, as if one were snoring.

From time to time I mingle with the Kolosh on the lake where they gather in great numbers on Sundays to watch the Russians ice skate and toboggan. Last Sunday after dinner we went to the lake. There were two sleds there, each one hitched to a horse. The ladies were driving along the lake in these sleds, because there is no other place to drive here. The Kolosh are dreadfully afraid of horses, and run headlong as soon as a horse goes near them. When the ladies had finished their drive, they invited us to a small inlet surrounded by firs. There on the ice they had laid a carpet, and on a table a samovar was boiling. For the first time in my life I had an opportunity to drink tea on ice. In the absence of other entertainment, this was fine. For the holiday they are preparing an amateur performance and are building a stage in the club. The good weather which began right when we arrived has not changed. The ice on the lake is good, and if it does not rain, then they will

CIVIL AND SAVAGE ENCOUNTERS

start to cut ice on Monday and load it on the ship. Then on Thursday, 22 December/3 January [1860/61] the ship, *Nakhimov*, will depart for California.

20 December 1860/1 January 1861

The weather held, and the ice was superb, with no slush; it was as sparkling and clear as crystal. Yesterday I went to the lake to watch them cutting ice. The operation is performed with marvelous ease and speed. A horse is harnessed to an iron cutter with one smooth runner and one with a sawtooth edge. The horse moves along at an even gait and the saw gouges the ice about two inches deep. Then they turn it back again and set the sledge so the smooth runner goes along the cut line and the saw cuts a new one. In this manner they mark the ice with absolutely straight lines and then cut lateral marks the same way. Thus they cut a large surface and mark it in perfectly uniform squares just like a checkerboard. Then along these marked lines they drag a saw-like plow, which cuts the ice eight inches thick. After that a single blow is enough to separate one block from the next. They heave these pieces up on the ice, and several Kolosh, who are barefoot as usual, pile up pieces one on top of another, and use a rope to drag them along wooden rails to the harbor.

I am astonished at the endurance of the Kolosh. They wear a blanket fastened under the chin which only comes down to their knees, at most, and they frequently do not even wear a shirt under this blanket. The Kolosh will work all day out on the ice in a costume such as this, when the temperature is 20°. Today I looked out of my window and saw a group of them bathing in the ocean, even children, and they stayed in the water for a long time, even with 7° of frost and a brisk wind. I gather they were freshening up after a celebration which was given for them by one of the toions who is building a new barabora. The celebration continued all night. Usually the building of a new barabora ends up by ruining the host. He builds the hut with the help of his relatives and friends, and pays them nothing for this, but when the barabora is finished, he must entertain all of them with an *igrushka* [potlatch]. This lasts for several days, until the host has nothing more to eat. He must also give presents to all his guests, and as a demonstration of his own wealth, he must destroy many of his own things. For example, during the feast yesterday at the toion's dwelling the host cut up 20 blankets into tiny pieces, and each of the blankets had cost six rubles. He also destroyed several pieces of calico and other things. It is understood that after such celebrations the host is quite ruined and must move into his new dwelling almost impoverished.

In former times when he destroyed his goods the host would also kill his slaves or *kalgas*, but this is not done now on Sitka. This is strictly supervised, and ends with the host giving the Company one slave, who in that moment becomes free, lives in New Arkhangel, and is maintained at Company expense. In exchange he does work for the Company. But among the Kolosh who live in the Sound, the custom of killing kalgas, especially during commemorations for the dead, continues right to the present time.

Yesterday we inspected the school where as many as 30 lads are being educated. They are the sons and orphans of promyshlenniks and of Company service personnel. These boys are educated at Company expense and are being prepared for various trades such as feldshers and scribes for offices. For this, upon completing their education, they must serve the Company for 10 years, of course at conventional wages. This school had been run down, but Furuhjelm rebuilt it at the first opportunity, and it is now quite satisfactory. Among the boys who study there, there is one little Kolosh lad who was designated to be killed during a celebration, but the owner gave him to the Company instead. The youngster is very bright and is already beginning to speak Russian quite well.

Today we are going to inspect the school for young girls. Furuhjelm wanted to build a small boarding school for girls here where, for a modest sum, daughters of service personnel, chinovniks and prikashchicks of the Company could study. Everything was ready, and they planned to appoint the wife of one

CIVIL AND SAVAGE ENCOUNTERS

Off the Oregon coast on the *Tsaritsa*, November 1860.

of the men here as head mistress. She had completed her schooling and has a governess certificate. She had asked Furuhjelm for this position, and he had agreed upon 500 silver rubles as her salary. But suddenly her lord and master informed her that he did not approve of the plan, and he seemed to be fiercely jealous of her, although she is not at all attractive. He keeps her locked up all the time now, and will not let her go out anywhere by herself, not even into the kitchen. He constantly sits in one room with her, and since such overseeing would be impossible if she took the post of head mistress of the school, he has emphatically rejected Furuhjelm's proposal. The poor woman weeps, but there is nothing to be done, and because there is no other head mistress, the boarding school remains only in the projected stage.

We have just returned from the girls' school; some 20 girls are being educated there; they are orphans, creoles, and there are several nonresidents. The girls learn God's commandments, reading, the four rules of arithmetic, handcrafts and cooking. They personally wash floors, also. In short, they are being prepared to be servants, or should they marry, to be the working wives of promyshlenniks of modest means. Everything appears to be going quite well. We asked that they introduce their best students to us, and then arranged that each should be given a new dress. All were given nuts, cakes and other such litle treats. Then there was an auction where various items the girls had made were sold. The money realized from such auctions is put into a special account, and the Company pays interest on it. When a girl marries or leaves the colonies, her share of the money is given to her. In this manner each one eventually receives from 100 to 150 silver rubles. The Company watches over their well-being for the duration of the time they are in the colonies, and from time to time issues money to them, or tries to find a position for them, or a suitable match. There were items of clothing for tiny children, and of course we tried to increase the amount of money taken in, so I bought some little knitted shirts, caps, baby clothes, tiny stockings and booties, and the like, for 40 silver rubles. Then I gave all the things I had bought to the midwife, a very nice person, to distribute to poor women in New Arkhangel. Kostlivtsov did the same.

We have excellent rapport with the Bishop here. He was also in the girls' school, and suggested to Furuhjelm that it might not be a bad idea to teach the young girls to sing in the choir in their free time. Furuhjelm found this a very fine idea, and right then and there instructed the priest to teach the girls to sing, so we hope to hear them some fine day in church, since the creoles usually have a good ear and like all kinds of singing. At dinner we learned that the little auction of baby clothes had raised more than 200 silver rubles for the school today.

After dinner we went to the lake to watch the ice being loaded. We met a Kolosh toion there, and this barefoot rascal was wearing a sable cloak worth at least 500 silver rubles over a dirty shirt. Some 50 Kolosh men and women were squatting barefoot around the area where the ice is being cut, silently observing the work. They will sit like that for three or four hours, then go out on the ice to play for a while, then again squat down and observe for several hours.

You will not be hearing from me for quite a while, because the next ship will not leave for California until May, so it will reach San Francisco at the same time we will, in the early part of June. I cannot foresee any other circumstances which will allow me to send a letter. I am going to try to hire a Kolosh to take letters to Stikine, near Sitka, from where they can be sent to the English colonies on Vancouver Island. There is regular communication from there with San Francisco. But it is really quite hopeless to send letters with the Kolosh, because the mail can so easily be lost. Thus you must expect only those letters which we ourselves will post in California at the beginning of June, which you will receive in late July or early August. Do not worry about this. Thank God I am healthy, and there is no reason why my health will be impaired. There is no reason to worry about us here. If only they had not delayed us in St. Petersburg, everything would be fine here.

Furuhjelm is a splendid man, straightforward and honest, who never speaks unkindly to anyone. Vn. [Voin Rimskii-Korsakov] lived with him for a long time on the Amur, knows him very well and can attest to my statement. A man such as Furuhjelm is a great asset to the Company, and they could not possibly find a finer man with a lantern. We heard that after our departure Company shares fell in price. Anyone would be an idiot to sell his shares. If I had any money I would immediately buy as many shares as I could, because I am convinced that I would make a great profit in a short time. It could easily be that the drop in the price of the shares is due to speculation on the part of some persons who wish to catch fish in muddy water. If this is so, they have really figured this very cleverly.

This afternoon Furuhjelm was informed that there is rumbling among the Kolosh. When the Kolosh are unhappy about anything, they assemble below the palisade which surrounds New Arkhangel and brandish their weapons and shout. It is an accepted fact here that, when the Kolosh are noisy, they are preparing some sort of unpleasantness. Furuhjelm immediately left to find out what the problem was. Apparently there had been a quarrel among the guests of the Russian toion Mikhailo in his barabora. One man grabbed another and stabbed him with a knife and wounded him slightly. The wounded man was a Sitka Kolosh, and the attacker was a Yakutat Kolosh. The quarrel grew, the Sitka Kolosh picked up their weapons and broke into Mikhailo's barabora to kill the Yakutats. The Yakutats rushed to the aid of their comrades. Within minutes the Kolosh of both parties had painted their faces red, which signifies their intention to battle; they had put on leather gauntlets and wooden slat armor, armed themselves with rifles and pistols, and were prepared to shoot each other. In fact, several men already had knife wounds. Obviously they could not be permitted to stab each other, right under the nose of the Russians, especially since blood vendettas begin after such incidents, and wars will go on, perhaps for several years, all along the shores of Russian America. In such a case all trade and relations with the Indians come to a halt. Consequently Furuhjelm immediately ordered that the cannon on the battery that faces the baraboras be elevated and that rockets be prepared. He informed the Kolosh that if they did not immediately disperse to their homes and cease rioting he would destroy the entire settlement. At first the Kolosh shouted that it was none of our business to interfere with their fights, and they started to brandish their weapons. But when they saw the cannon being elevated, they rushed off to their baraboras as fast as they could, since they knew that Furuhjelm abides by his word implicitly. Thus the dispute ended, and tomorrow, with the assistance of our intermediaries, payments to the wounded in the form of money and blankets will commence. Thus we will avoid a blood vengeance.

22 December 1860/3 January 1861

What do you think caused the quarrel among the Kolosh yesterday? It is a very simple matter. A year ago, during one of the celebrations, the Sitka Kolosh *outsang* the Yakutat Kolosh. I must explain that during the celebrations there is always a singing period, when they beat the drum and dance. It seems that the Sitka Kolosh knew more songs than the Yakutats, so the Yakutats had to be silent and listen while the Sitkas were singing, and they found this very vexing. Consequently, during the summer the Yakutats sent several men to the Copper River and north to other Indians to learn new songs, so that during the winter celebrations they would not have to take a second place to the Sitkas. Well, during the first celebrations, whatever song the Sitkas would start to sing, the Yakutats would pick up and sing and dance right along with them. The Yakutats had already agreed in advance that in case the Sitkas should outsing them, they would attack and kill them to avenge their humiliation. For this reason they came to the celebrations armed, but since the Sitkas were unaware of this agreement, they regarded this as a usual matter. Yesterday they had a celebration at the dwelling of the toion Aleksandr, who had built a new barabora. At first everything went along well, they sang and

CIVIL AND SAVAGE ENCOUNTERS

danced around the clock. Then suddenly the Sitkas started to sing an Aleut song, and the Yakutats were open-mouthed. When they had sent their men to learn songs from the Indians, it hadn't occurred to them that the Aleuts sing, too. The humiliation was clear, and without a second's pause, they fired their guns and revolvers at the Sitkas, and fell on them with their knives.

The unarmed Sitkas could not defend themselves, and they all probably would have been killed, if one woman had not knocked out two boards from the barabora with her axe. The Sitkas escaped out onto the street through this opening, and two or three minutes later returned armed to avenge their comrades. At just that moment Furuhjelm appeared and stopped further bloodshed, as I wrote to you earlier. Then several of the toions brought out the headgear and hunting hats of some of the famous toions who had been killed some time previously. In the names of the dead they demanded, while singing their war songs, that everyone put down his weapons and have a 24–hour peace, and then they could discuss matters and decide whether to continue the war or to conclude the matter peacefully.

Today accurate facts have been gathered, and it appears that thirteen Sitka men have been wounded, three of them so seriously that the Kolosh, contrary to custom, did not turn to the shamans for help but asked our doctor to help the wounded. One of the wounded had two bullets in his chest, another had been stabbed in the abdomen and all of his intestines had extruded, and the third had been hit on the head by a wooden instrument resembling a flail, which is used to kill sea lions. He had been hit so hard that the poor man, in spite of the fact that he had had a wooden hat on his head, still has not regained consciousness, and he is hemorrhaging from the mouth. This wounded man is the host himself, the toion Aleksandr, who gave the party. There were five Yakutats wounded, but none seriously.

None of this would matter if it were not for the fact that by Kolosh custom blood demands blood, or at least payment for blood. Perhaps they will be able to settle the matter so that everyone who was wounded will be compensated properly either by payment in money, or by goods, or by slaves. But in case anyone dies, and this must be expected, any payment will be too high for the Yakutats to be able to pay, and then the Sitkas will have the right to kill one Yakutat for every dead Sitka. Then the Yakutats will take vengeance on the Sitkas, and then the Sitkas on the Yakutats. Other tribes will become involved in the quarrel, relatives of one or the other side, and the killing will go on for several years.

Furuhjelm informed the Kolosh that he is ordering them to terminate this affair peacefully, and if they decide to take vengeance, he will personally intervene in their quarrel; under no circumstances will he allow them to kill one another. The Sitkas have replied that they are ready to make peace, as soon as the Yakutats have paid the indemnity and have left the island. Negotiations still have not been concluded. If the Yakutats agree to everything demanded of them, then that will be the end of the affair. If, however, they refuse to leave the island, then force will have to be used. A ship will have to be sent to burn their baraboras and then kill any who will not comply. The hope is that the affair will not reach that stage, and that a threat alone will be enough to bring the Yakutats into submission. There are 150 men and their families. Our settlement is certainly completely safe, and the 60 guns and local garrison are fully adequate to hold down any attempt by all the Kolosh united together.

I have been describing this incident to you in order to illustrate what animals these savages are, and what insignificant causes are enough to start internecine battles in which more than 100 may be killed. Now they have just announced to us that the quarrel among the Kolosh has been satisfactorily concluded. The Yakutats have agreed to pay the indemnity, and tomorrow they will leave here with their families to go back to their own homes. Bon Voyage!

In spring we will be dealing with people who are the exact opposites of the Kolosh. These are the Aleuts, who inhabit all the islands of the Aleutian chain. From everything we have managed to learn about the Aleuts up to now, from tales and descriptions, it is apparent that they are very kind and peaceful people. However, it is also evident from various accounts that before they were conquered by the Russians, the Aleuts had been quite brave and warlike. From time to time the inhabitants of one island attacked those of another, and these quarrels killed a great number of their people.

When the Russians subjugated the Aleutian Islands, the discords were ended, but the poor Aleuts were forced for a long time to suffer a bitter fate. At first everything went rather well, but lawless Russian promyshlenniks exploited the meekness and naiveté of the Aleuts for evil purposes. The desire to free themselves from the foreign yoke induced the Aleuts to attack and destroy several of our promyshlennik ships, and to kill all the Russians. They thought that by killing the crews of these ships they would be rid of their oppressors forever. But in the spring of the next year new Russian promyshlenniks would appear to avenge their murdered comrades, and there was no end to their excesses. Over the course of several years, they killed Aleuts by every possible means. Especially notorious in this regard were Glotov and Solovev, or Solovei, as he was known, and their associates. They wiped out whole settlements. They would drive unarmed Aleuts into their iurts with wives and children, and set fire to them; then they would knock down the iurts and suffocate the people inside. Sometimes they would spare a few young Aleut girls and boys to serve as slaves. Solovei would amuse himself by standing 12 Aleuts in a line, one behind another, and firing a gun at them to see in which Aleut the bullet would lodge. He learned through experience that the bullet would pass through nine and lodge in the tenth. Little by little, however, these excesses were ended.

Now the Aleuts are very meek; in fact, one can say they are a disspirited people. They govern themselves through elected toions or elders. All their disagreements are settled by the group or *mir*.* Our laws are completely foreign to them, and there is no need to apply them to the Aleuts. They do not commit murder, and theft is quite unknown. Women and young

---

*mir,the Community. Golovin suggests that the Aleuts had a pattern of community resolution similar to that in rural Russia, where the system of *mir* or *obshchestvo*(society) prevailed.—Eds.

girls are not known for their chastity, but the Russians are partly to blame for this, having convinced then that chastity is a vice, not a virtue.

The Aleuts are hospitable and generous. When an Aleut returns from a fishing trip, he puts his catch on the shore and goes home. Then anyone who needs fish can come and take what he needs, and the owner of the fish will make do with what is left. They have all been baptized, attend church zealously, and fulfill all their obligations; but this does not indicate their dedication to orthodoxy. If the Turks were to seize control of the Aleutian Islands tomorrow, and order the Aleuts to become Mohammedans, the Aleuts would oblige, and with a murmur they would zealously start reading the Koran and attend mosques, just as they presently read the Gospel and go to church. In general, they are all very lazy and heedless. They almost have to be forced to procure the necessary amount of fish for themselves for winter, and prevented from foolishly squandering this supply, for otherwise they would just eat it all, and not stop until they had finished up everything. They eat, sleep, and eat again.

It is only six months since I left Russia, and I have already seen so much, and will see much more in the days ahead. Everything is interesting and diverting, but all the same the words of [Ivan A.] Krylov often come to mind:

Be assured that you will never find a better land
Than where your loved one and your friend do dwell.

And I am impatient for the moment when I will be with you again, my dear ones . . .

New Arkhangel   8/20 January 1861

I do not yet know how and when I will send this letter to you, but for your peace of mind I hope it will be sent from Sitka before we set out to inspect the colonies. We had thought of setting up a postal service using the Kolosh, but these hostile children, God forgive me, are so preoccupied with their internecine quarrels, and are so lazy, that there is no possibility of persuading them to budge from their places. The one hope is that the freeze, which started again on the evening of 5 January, will continue four more days. Then it will be possible to cut 400 tons of ice, which with the amount already cut, will amount to 1,200 tons, which is a full load for the ship *Tsaritsa*. In that case the ship would be sent to California at the end of February or the beginning of March, since the ship *Nakhimov*, which took our previous letters, will be back by that time. Of course, March is still a long way off, but from time to time I will be adding to this letter, and in this way we will be having a chat in absentia.

For the first time I will tell you how I have been passing the time from the departure of *Nakhimov* up until now. On Christmas we went to the service in the cathedral, and then paid a visit to the Bishop. I must tell you that the cathedral here is cold, with no heat whatsoever, so that during the service, when it is freezing outside, there is no way to avoid being cold. The Bishop himself performed the service wearing rubber overshoes. But there is nothing to be done! Usually I go to the service, after prayers I go up to the cross, and then when the Bishop takes off his vestments, I go up for his blessing and kiss his hand. Then we all go to have breakfast at his house. We spent the evening of the first day of the holidays at Furuhjelm's, where there was a Christmas tree.

The theatrical performances began on the 26th [of December]. The theater was organized by amateurs from the service personnel of the third class who are serving in the colonies: this includes minor prikashchiks, office scribes, et cetera. The female roles were taken by the widow of a boatswain and the wife of one of the promyshlenniks. The theater is located in the club. In the morning there were dress rehearsals to which the general public were admitted, but only dignitaries [*pochetnykh*] and semi-dignitaries were allowed to attend the evening performance. In both instances the price of a ticket was one paper ruble per performance. Kostlivtsov and I paid 25 paper rubles for all three performances, and made an appearance every evening to encourage the talent.

Two of the actors, Lebedev and Churkin, were quite good. The latter is a relative of a *gostinnyi dvor** merchant; he is a very talented fellow who works as a clerk in the Chief Administrator's office; but he is a terrible drunkard. In order not to ruin the play in which Churkin was one of the main characters, they had to put him in a cell every day after the performance. Even then, when all the performances were over, he was dead drunk for 24 hours. They performed *The Surly Man, The Confused Man, The Kharkov Fiancé, Lordly Arrogance, Narrow Boots* and *The Everyday Uniform*. We shouted with laughter at these performances. The actors often made absolutely terrible mistakes. For example, one actor who was praising his bride, stated, "This, my brother, is truly a *medicinal Venus* [meaning Venus de Medici]!" Another, explaining that the groom had locked up his fiancée, stated, "This young fellow spoiled [meaning locked up] his bride!" The third said, "To show disrespect to one's leader, well, do you know what this is? This, my little father, is crinoline [meaning criminal]!" And finally, this same person called one young fellow an Apollo of Beloozersk [meaning Belvedere], obviously as a complement to the medicinal Venus. There were several other slips, but it would be indecent to write them down.

All this time we have had the same good weather which we had the very day we arrived; then on the 27th it changed, and a brisk wind came up and there was a driving rain, which, however, did not prevent the local inhabitants from their merry-making, going along from house to house wearing masks, of course on foot because there are no carriages here except two homemade sleds which are used to drive around the lake. We also went to the theater on the 28th, and then spent the evening with some of the local dignitaries. There were tremendous thunderstorms on the nights of December 30 and January 2, especially the latter, when there were thunder and lightning all night long. There are no thunderstorms here at all in the summer. We spent New Year's in the club, and quite by chance, on the water, since a very nice

*A primitive "shopping center" in Russia, where many merchants gathered under one roof to sell their goods. Russian officials supervised to be certain taxes were paid on all trade.—Eds.

CIVIL AND SAVAGE ENCOUNTERS

display of fireworks had been set up in front of the club windows, set to go off just at 12:00; and after our fireworks display, the heavenly fireworks started, and thunder rumbled in the mountains for more than an hour. By 5:00 AM it was very quiet, but overcast. At night the thermometer dropped sharply; then at 9:00 AM it started to rise again. At 11:00 AM there was a squall out of the northwest with snow which became a fierce hurricane. All the ships in the harbor were dragged with their anchors. The *Tsaritsa* broke her chain and was tossed up on shore, but fortunately with no damage. The hurricane was so bad it was impossible to keep one's footing. Our house up on the heights shook right down to the foundations. The windows seemed ready to blow out at any moment. Fortunately the wind moderated after midday, and by 4:00 PM it was almost completely still. Then it started to freeze, and by the next day, Epiphany, it was clear and the sun shone through the frost, and the temperature was 10°. The freeze still continues. Thanks to the good weather we have resumed our daily walks to the Kolosh River. Only one thing bothers me, and that is having to walk up our wretched stairs of 80 overly wide high steps!

In order to thank local society for many kindnesses, Kostlivtsov and I are giving a ball on Sunday, January 15, and we have invited the entire population of Sitka. Because of this I am constantly bustling about with the cook these days, and trying to put together the necessary supplies for dessert and for supper. It is very difficult to get anything good here, and you cannot imagine how expensive it all is. However, I hope that everything will be all right, and that we will manage for not over 200 silver rubles. The Sitka gossip-mongers will compose a chronology from this marvelous event.

Recently peace has been concluded between the warring Kolosh. They were quiet for a long time, but were not in agreement on the conditions. Finally, on the third [of January] Furuhjelm sent a bark armed with cannon to sail along the Kolosh settlement, and by way of a lesson, ordered several blank charges to be fired. This did it. The very next morning the Kolosh began to exchange hostages, and after the noon meal they fired off their guns and revolvers as a sign of peace. Only one toion, Aleksandr, who had done everything as ordered, suddenly decided to demand a special payment for himself, to compensate for the beating to which he had been subjected during the skirmish. Aleksandr has a very strong influence over the Kolosh, who do not like him, but fear him very much because he thinks nothing of killing a man, and is already quite advanced in age. Fearing that Aleksandr's demands might cause new outbursts, Furuhjelm ordered that he be told that if he did not stop stirring up trouble he would have no hesitation in having him killed like a dog. The Kolosh know very well that Furuhjelm keeps his word, and so they have finally calmed down and are now back at work in the harbor. Others have gone out after fish and iaman which they did not bring into the market at all during the period of strife.

13/25 January 1861

In spite of the fact that the weather has changed since the evening of the 10th, and the rain has been coming down by the bucketful, nevertheless yesterday they managed to finish cutting ice on the lake and now have the requisite amount to send to California. This means there is hope that *Tsaritsa* will sail from here at the end of February or beginning of March, which would mean that you would receive this letter by the end of May or the early part of June.

On the 10th, Tuesday, we watched some Kolosh dances. There were 30 men dancing, and several women, but the women do not actually take part in the dancing. They just sing with a group of men and stand apart and clap their hands. The dancers were all arrayed in the costumes they usually wear for such occasions. These costumes are handed down from one generation to the next, and it is impossible to describe them adequately. The chief components are the blankets, which are white, red, green, blue or yellow, either plain or decorated with various designs such as stars, faces, et cetera. These blankets are worn over both

CIVIL AND SAVAGE ENCOUNTERS

shoulders like a cape. Under the blankets they wear shirts of various colors, and their legs are mostly bare. Instead of blankets some wear animal pelts such as bear, fox, sable or ermine. On their heads they wear grass hats of a special design, and some wear their hair gathered into a topknot, into which they tie twigs which protrude above the head and resemble a tall narrow work basket. Others wear *scalps* on top of their hair; these are hair, together with skin, which they have taken from the heads of dead enemies. In short, anything can be worn on the head. All of this is covered with a thick layer of down, so that when they dance it blows off like snow in the air. Their faces are decorated with various designs, the stranger the better, but only with black and red pigments. One man had painted a huge red star over his entire face, which was covered with a thick layer of black paint. Another had painted his entire physiognomy with wavy black and red lines; a third, dressed to look like a bear, painted his face black and made a wide red circle around his mouth, and painted his eyebrows red. If you met someone like this in the forest at night, you could be frightened to death. Each person has rattles in his hands, of all shapes and sizes, but most were small and round, with the beaks of sea parrots attached; this bird is known here by the name of *toporok*.

All of these people gathered on the battery near the harbor and wailed a most savage song to the beat of the drums. Then together they started to jump in rhythm in a weirdly twisting and tortuous fashion. The louder the song and the more contorted their bodies, the better. The barefoot dancers were oblivious to the snow and frost, and carried on remarkably—this was a dance of forest spirits, something wild and frenzied. The more they danced the more excited they became. The dance intoxicates them, and those who participate gradually reach a state of such unrestrained madness that they are ready to dance for several hours at a time. During such times murders take place. It is quite common to go from dancing to murder.

We watched this saturnalia for about an hour and then left the Kolosh, ordered that both men and women be given a charka of vodka each, and they moved along to their baraboras, continuing their songs and frenzy for a still longer time. I neglected to mention that almost all the Kolosh wear rings in their noses. During the dance they remove the rings and instead they insert feathers of various lengths, slender sticks, whale and sea lion whiskers and the like. It is very picturesque . . .

16/28 January 1861

Yesterday we gave our ball; I wrote to you earlier about the preparations for it. A week beforehand invitations were sent out to the guests. With the exception of notorious drunkards, all distinguished individuals and their families and households were invited. On the eve of the ball a well-fed bull calf was slaughtered, so as not to have to feed the guests wild goat. We had also sent out men at our own expense to bring in halibut, and they had about a pud and a half [54 pounds]. Last evening at 6:30 our quarters were lighted with two candelabra; two rows of lampions were lighted on the main street from one end of the village to the other; similar lamps were placed on the steps leading to our house and along the palisaded fence surrounding the building; and along the shore they lit barrels of oil. The scene was really not bad. Precisely at 7:00 the guests appeared. Because of the dearth of musicians on Sitka, and because the local ones are quite bad, we had moved a poor old fortepiano into the hall, as well as a decent organ, and a splendid grand piano which belongs to Madame Furuhjelm. However, for the most part we danced to the accompaniment of the fortepiano and a violin which was constantly bothered by strings breaking, and had to be tuned after almost every piece. But we became accustomed to this. During the entr'acte between dances Mesdames Furuhjelm and Maksutova, both excellent musicians, played several pieces on the grand piano, so that we had both a dance and a concert.

The ball opened with a Polish dance, and then quadrilles, waltzes, polkas and others followed in their turn. There were some extremely amusing guests, such as a man named Fld., who is a ship's mechanic; he is an old man of about 60, and is tall, skinny and gangling. He is married to a woman he picked up in Hamburg, and in spite of the fact that she is about 50 and not very attractive, he is as jealous of her as any Othello. She is permitted to dance only with her husband, and he will not give anyone a chance to flatter his other half. Such a skinny old fellow, tall as can be—he dances everything, quadrilles, polkas, waltzes, mazurkas. He does not spare his feet, and all this to make certain his wife is not bored and does not get it into her head to dance with another partner, even as a courtesy in case someone has the unfortunate notion of asking her to dance. Everyone has become used to them, but I cannot look at this couple without laughing. Last night during one of the quadrilles, the partner who was leading decided to turn the next figure into a cotillion. The old man, Fld., who was dancing with his wife, at first smiled in approval, watching the whriling dancers. But then his turn came, and as the figure began with five couples, he realized he would be separated from his wife, who was seized by the local doctor. Fld. had to dance with a young girl. You should have seen how his face fell, how terribly funny he looked, trying to dance the polka with his partner. And on top of this, when the doctor had finished the turn, he took Madame Fld. to a corner of the room and hid her with his body, so that the frantic husband could not see where she was. I was literally exploding with laughter. Finally the wife took mercy on her husband and went up to him. The face of the old man instantly became radiant, and he regarded his wife with such affection! When we leave here, we will have the pleasure of her company when we are at sea, because when we leave, under no circumstances will Fld. leave his wife behind on shore. He even wanted to include this as a condition of his contract. When he is aboard the ship he keeps her in the boiler room and will not let her out on deck even for a moment.

There is also a nice creole woman, T---a, a midwife, who is an old woman of about 50, but she is merry and dances and is amusing. She has three grown daughters whose faces are the color of unpolished brown boots. *J'aime beaucoup cette femme sage et aimable; la providence des dames de Sitka*, who actually do try to fulfill the commandment to multiply and be fruitful! There were several other unique personalities, but it would take too long to describe them all. We danced a great deal, because the creole women like to dance very much; this and their attire are their only pastimes. Laziness has developed among them to such a degree that any mental or physical work is a burden to them. Consequently very few of the creole women know how to read. One woman, who is still young and rather attractive, married a quite well-educated man two years ago, but it was only recently, and by chance, that she learned that Jesus Christ and the Savior are one and the same. Until then, she had supposed that Jesus Christ was one person, and the Savior another.

The lack of any activity, plus the savage blood which courses in the veins of these creole women, is the reason that although maidens somehow maintain their chastity, once they are married, in a month or two they cast caution to the winds. Of course there are exceptions, but they are rare. The creoles themselves say that to marry a creole woman means to take a wife for others to enjoy. One young man married a creole woman and, during a dance on the day of their wedding some of his friends began to tease him, so he declared he would bet his life that his young wife was still a virgin. "Hey, brother," responded the father of the bride, "don't part with your head. I am her very own father, but even I cannot make such a guarantee for a creole woman!" After he marries, a creole man pays little attention to what his wife does, and submits to fate without a murmur. Among the lower classes of creoles, husbands calmly peddle their wives' favors, maintaining that since one cannot rely on their fidelity, it is better to reap some benefit from the infidelity. In exchange for a bottle or two of rum, a man will give his wife's services for a day or two or a week, depending on the terms. This is done openly, a quite ordinary occurrence.

Rum and vodka play an important role here. The free sale of spirits is prohibited, in order to curb drunkenness. Spirits can be purchased only from the Company, and there are many restrictions. Creoles and others are generally addicted to drink, and

116   *CIVIL AND SAVAGE ENCOUNTERS*

New Arkhangel (Sitka), the capital of Russian America.

since they have difficulty in getting vodka from the Company, at least in the quantities they would like, they try to obtain it from other inhabitants, to whom it is supplied freely from the warehouse. Therefore, in spite of the prohibitions, all work here is valued in terms of spirits. A shoemaker, for example, will ask 25 or 30 paper rubles for one pair of boots, but if you give him rum instead of money, then for the same pair of boots, he will be satisfied with one bottle of rum, which costs 3.50 paper rubles in the warehouse. It is understood that everyone who can will pay for work with spirits rather than with money. However, we are getting away from the ball.

First of all the guests were served tea, then confections, preserves, dried raisins, prunes and almonds, since there are no other desserts here. Then they were given ice cream. At 10:00, according to the local custom, they were served light appetizers, then sweets again, and at 12:00 we sat down to supper, the ladies in the sitting room and the gentlemen in my room. There were 75 guests in all. While the guests were eating supper, the candles were replaced in the hall, and after supper the dancing started again and continued until 3:00 in the morning. According to all accounts, it seems that everyone was most pleased, and had a wonderful time. The ball gave the people here a subject for conversation for several weeks at least, and it certainly has diverted them from the gossip caused by our arrival. And finally, it demonstrated to everyone our several peaceful intentions, and this was what we needed.

16/28 February 1861

We have spent the past month in our usual manner—most of the time we have been working or discussing the condition of the colonies with various persons. In the evenings we sometimes go to the club or pay a call on someone. God only knows what these evenings are like. People come together at 6:00 and break up at 9:00 or 9:30, so that when you come home you don't know what to do with yourself. You don't want to work, it's too early to go to bed, and it is simply very depressing. The weather has been mostly bad, with rain, snow, hail, fog, and at times thunder; only rarely has the sun been out. But in spite of this we go for walks whenever possible, and during good weather we may go for two or three walks a day. There were a few days when it was almost too warm to wear an overcoat while walking.

I really love to go out into the forest about three versts from New Arkhangel. The forest begins right at the harbor, and there is a little path which leads through the woods to a stream where there used to be a small Russian settlement which the Kolosh destroyed in 1855. It used to be too dangerous to go into the forest, for fear of being attacked by the Kolosh, but now everyone goes to this stream, and in fact they go unarmed. The forest is really magnificent! If you go off the path it is almost impossible to move through the dense thicket, and you can only go a short distance. The backwoods area is beyond description. Centuries-old trees, felled by the wind, lie one atop another. Some have already rotted and turned into loam; others disintegrate at a touch, and new trees grow on top of these fallen giants, not infrequently as much as 90 feet in height. It is a truly picturesque place, especially in summer, when raspberries grow all over these stumps, with immense but watery berries, and flowers blossom so that their nectar and pollen attract thousands of hummingbirds. Where do all these tiny birds come from? Why do they come to Sitka where the flowers have no scent, and fruits have no flavor or aroma? I am usually accompanied on my strolls by two enormous dogs. One is a Newfoundland named Polkan, black as tar, and the other is Maklak, a dark brown Siberian breed. When they see me coming, each picks up the first stick he can find and then they triumphantly bring them to me. All along our walk they run along ahead of me, snatching up sticks and stones which I throw for them, and chase away all the little pigs and cows they meet. They can swim far out into the sea very well, struggling against the surf, and they return home altogether content with their walk, each carrying a stick in his mouth. Little by little they have filled a whole corner in the club corridor with these sticks.

Yesterday there was a wedding of the local school supervisor, a very young and modest chap, who married a pretty young creole girl . . .

3/15 March 1861

Now we are in the month of March, Lent has begun, and the ship *Nakhimov* has still not returned from California. We are impatiently awaiting news from our families. The weather is bad, with rain, snow, hail, and, just for variety, fog and storms. I am still thankful that from time to time some incident or other occurs, so that we are occasionally diverted. For example, this is what happened on the third.

There is a magnetic observatory here on Sitka, and there is a director at the observatory. He is an official from the Academy of Sciences, who was sent here about a year ago. His name is Knplts.; he is Polish, and has a wife and a small daughter. He is still not an old man. He has been married for 11 years, and his wife is not especially pretty, but this does not stop him from being violently jealous of her. It is strange that the young men are less jealous than the older family men. He has made life a real hell for his wife ever since her arrival on Sitka. He never goes out anywhere. His assistant works at the observatory while he stays at home all the time, where he fusses about with cipher after cipher and plagues his wife. If she goes into another room or into the kitchen, he is right behind her. He looks everywhere, under the divan, under a bench, under the table, to make certain no one is hiding there to captivate his wife. The windows are always bolted and the curtains are drawn. The wife and daughter can talk to each other only in whispers. Loud conversation is prohibited under threat of beating. At night he personally locks the outside door with a key and a bolt. The door to the sitting room is likewise locked with a key, and he puts a silver spoon on the handle so that if anyone tampers with the lock the spoon will fall and the noise will awaken him. The next door is also locked, and he hangs an iron and other things against the door. Finally, the door into the bedroom is locked with a key and is tied up with wire, and then he hangs a blanket over it. All the curtains are drawn and fastened with pins, so there will be no chink to peek through, and the shutters are closed, too.

You can imagine the situation of this poor woman who is always locked in and has to listen to his unending curses. She is frequently beaten, and all day long she does not dare to talk or move! When they came to Sitka, they were assigned quarters on a small island, Iaponskii, opposite the harbor and right near the observatory. But Knplts. found these quarters uncomfortable and put his assistant there, so that he could move to the harbor. When he is taken with a fit of jealousy he sometimes becomes violent. Once he broke all the glass in his house—every bit. The doctor, who knows the domestic situation there, told this whole story to Furuhjelm's assistant, Prince Maksutov, who was at that time taking over as Chief Administrator during Furuhjalm's absence. Maksutov personally went with the doctor to see Knplts, because the wife was complaining about the barbaric treatment. The doctor firmly declared that Knplts. was insane, and said that he must go to the hospital to be treated. At first he did not want to do this, but at last he agreed, and was put in a special room in the hospital. His wife and daughter breathed freely. Then Furuhjelm returned, and when he learned everything that had happened, he invited Madame Knplts. to his own home, questioned her, introduced her to his wife, and in an effort to give her financial assistance, since they had very limited means, he offered her a position as the head of the local school for girls, of course with an appropriate salary. The poor woman was ecstatic. In such a situation she could live at the school and be free from her husband's tyranny. She could live comfortably there. And it would be a good thing for the local people because Madame Knplts. is a very modest, sensible, well-educated woman, and could be a fine teacher. But suddenly her lord and master returned home peacefully after 10 days in the hospital, announced to his wife that thank God he had regained his

CIVIL AND SAVAGE ENCOUNTERS

health, and that she had done enough flitting about without him. She told him about Furuhjelm's offer to her and he said she could not even consider it. When Furuhjelm asked his consent he replied that *his wife was his chattel,* and that no one had any business with her.

Meanwhile the intervention of Maksutov and Furuhjelm and the interest which other local people were taking in his wife led Knplts. to conclude that all of these gentlemen were lusting after her. From that moment he began to consider Maksutov, Furuhjelm and the local office administrator, Lindenberg, a married man with five children, as his prime enemies. Even mentioning the names of these gentlemen would send him into a rage. When we first arrived on Sitka, Furuhjelm told us about his intention to open the school for girls, which he considered an absolute necessity, and stated that his proposal must be carried out in spite of Knplts.' jealousy and stupidity. We advised Furuhjelm to convince Knplts. that he was being ridiculous, but the latter would not come to Furuhjelm; he only sent a stupid reply and said he wanted to be left in peace. He later came to us to complain that he was being persecuted, and when we tried to point out to him that he was persecuting himself, his wife and their child, and that he would certainly eventually be the death of them, his jealousy even extended to us.

During this time his wife's situation became almost unbearable and she was unable to do anything. For six months she did not set foot outside her house or have a breath of fresh air. More than once she contemplated running away from her husband, but he would not let her out of his sight. Finally on 1 March, for the first time in his life, he decided to take a nap after his midday meal. Scarcely had he fallen asleep when his wife grabbed the child and a small bundle which she had secretly prepared, and rushed out onto the street, then ran as fast as she could to Madame Lindenberg, asking for refuge and protection. Knplts. woke up at the very moment when she left, and he started to look for her in the kitchen and other room, and finally ran out after her; but she was already far away. Then the enraged husband ran to Maksutov's home, where he snatched up some rocks and threw them through the window of

Maksutov's house, then ran back to his own house. Maksutov was asleep at the time, and his wife, who was expecting a child, fortunately was not at home. You can imagine Maksutov's astonishment when the rocks came crashing in on him through the broken glass. At first he thought perhaps the Kolosh had burst into the settlement. God only knows what else went through his mind. Then as he went up to the window he suddenly caught sight of Knplts. running off; he hadn't even thought of him.

The wife of K. is now living at the Lindenbergs' until her husband is sent back to the hospital. She visited us and told us about her situation, and really, it breaks your heart just to look at this poor woman. They have put a guard over her husband in order to prevent him from causing further problems. He is quite out of his mind and claims that he was not arrested by a proper administrator, but by Maksutov, and that all of this is a conspiracy. "They took my wife away from me, and sent me to the hospital. I expected that this would happen. But these men are all old libertines, married, with scandalously decadent morals." He is certain that he is right, and that he did just the right thing in breaking Maksutov's window in revenge for everything he has endured. However he is letting his wife petition for a divorce, and even travel to California; but he cannot accept the idea that she is free, that she lives with the Lindenbergs and goes to see Madame Furuhjelm. We laughed a great deal about this whole story, especially about all the precautions K. took every night. Sometimes he would go to bed very late and his wife and daughter would have to sit up until he retired, since they had to hand him the spoon, the iron, the bolts, and everything else he needed to construct his barricades.

11/23 March 1861

Finally on the evening of the 9th the long-awaited bark *Nakhimov* returned from California and brought us news from

home, including your letters to me, my dear Maman and Soeur P.,
dated 24 September and 13 and 30 October.

14/26 March 1861

My conversation with you was interrupted, my dear ones, and
now here I am again taking pen in hand three days later. On
Sunday I went to Mass, which, by the way, went on for three hours,
thanks to a Requiem and the Bishop's sermon. After Mass we all
went to the harbor to see the Kolosh, who were armed as if they
were set for war, lay siege to one of the small islands in their small
boats which they call *lodkas*. All had painted their faces black and
red, and they were all armed with guns, pistols and knives. Their
costumes had great variety. In the prow of each boat sat a man
wearing a hat made from the head of some animal such as a bear,
wolf, sea lion, et cetera. There was no small amount of shouting,
noise and gunfire. At the end, all of them were given a charka of
vodka and went back home very much satisfied.

Yesterday I spent the whole day on correspondence and only
managed to take my walk in the forest in the morning. Today at
7:00 AM we went out about 20 miles on a ship, first to the sulphur
springs where there used to be a medical treatment structure which
was destroyed by the Kolosh about seven years ago. These springs
are located on the shore of a very picturesque bay. As we walked
toward the spring we noticed that there was a fire on shore, with
people walking about. The Kolosh come from various places to
stay here. Furuhjelm, Kostlivtsov and I got into a little rowboat and
set out for the place where we could see the fire burning. As we
approached, several armed Kolosh came out of the forest. We
pulled up on shore, jumped out of the boat and went right over to
them. It appeared that these were Sitka Kolosh, some of whom live
at the springs in huts while they are recovering from various
ailments, and others had come to hunt. When they saw us they put
down their weapons and guided us to the springs.

When we had inhaled an abundance of sulphur, I gave one of the Kolosh women a cigar, and then we returned to the ship and set out for the Ozersk Redoubt, which had been designated for catching and salting fish, and is somewhat protected from the danger of attack by the Kolosh. The entire garrison consists of seven workers and two women, and an Arab belonging to Prince Menshikov who for some unknown reason has been sent to Sitka to be reformed. And in fact, the Ozersk Redoubt, in spite of its beautiful location, is an excellent place of exile: impermeable backwoods, far away from the entire world, with no way to buy even vodka.

After we had seen the redoubt we inspected the superb Serebriannikov Bay. It penetrates the interior of the island for about five miles, and winds like a river between high mountains covered with ancient forests. In the interior a splendid waterfall cascades down from a great height. It is wild, but marvelously beautiful—a splendid backdrop for the wolf's ravine in *Freischutz*. I examined this bay, selecting a place where naval cruisers and Company ships could be hidden in case of war. In New Arkhangel these are completely unprotected, and Serebriannikov Bay could be easily and superbly fortified so the enemy could never take it. When we had finished our inspection we returned home at 7:00 PM. The weather was excellent, quiet, clear; but when we returned it was quite cold. By the way, chère Maman, you were asking whether there is no winter on Sitka? There is winter, but the sea never freezes, and navigation is open the year around . . .

18/30 March 1861

Yesterday the men started loading ice aboard the ship *Tsaritsa*. In about three days the loading will be completed, and *Tsaritsa* will set out for San Francisco with our letters, and soon we will be on our way. We will be sailing aboard the steam clipper *Aleksandr II*, a beautiful and very fast new ship. The weather is usually good here in April and May, so it will not be like the fall and winter sailing when the storms blow without any letup. Furuhjelm and his secretary will be sailing with us, so the voyage will be interesting. The journey from California to New York will also be at a good time of year, and since there are not usually very many passengers from California, I hope we will have a more peaceful time than on the *Washington*, and of course the food will be better. The voyage to Europe will also be good, and when we set foot on European soil, we will consider ourselves home. We still do not know how we will make our way to Europe, whether through England or directly to France; but in either case we will go to Paris.

31 March/12 April 1861

This letter was long since signed, sealed and delivered to the office, and it was even put aboard *Tsaritsa*, but you know the proverb, "Man proposes, God disposes," and it has been returned to me. Naturally I am taking this opportunity to add a few more lines and let you know more recent news about myself. Do you want to know why this letter was not sent as scheduled? The matter is very simple. The ship which was towing *Tsaritsa* out to sea did not take her through the usual channel and grounded her on the rocks. Half an hour later she was back out at sea, but leaked so seriously she had to be towed back into port and hauled up on shore in order to keep her from sinking. Then they had to throw the ice overboard and completely unload her. This whole operation will take no small amount of time, so they are now preparing the bark *Nakhimov* for sailing. She is being loaded with ice, of which there is still fortunately a surplus in the ice house, and she will probably put out to sea on Wednesday, 5 April, carrying our letters. That same day after our noon dinner we will leave Sitka.

The incident with *Tsaritsa* was actually not very serious, but nevertheless it interrupted all the plans which had been made for the sailing of Company ships for the rest of this year. Fortunately it is still possible to remedy everything, and we have personally offered to help Furuhjelm, because this occurrence has worried him very much. I must tell you that Furuhjelm is an outstanding man, and a Chief Administrator whose equal the Company could not easily find. He has been governing the colonies since 1859, and is so concerned about everything that it is a pleasure to see how eagerly he supervises all those things that have been assigned to him, and is quick to correct mistakes of the past. Up to now everything has gone as smoothly as a hot knife through butter, and he had thought that by sending three cargoes of ice to California on *Tsaritsa* he would receive $50,000, so that he would then be in a position to do something useful for the colonies and make a substantial profit for the Company. Suddenly the incident with *Tsaritsa* has taken more than half that sum from him, and has ruined all his plans. He suggested taking us to Kodiak and remaining there, then when the ship took us to California it would return for him and take him on a tour through the Northern Department of the colonies and return to Sitka by October. But now the repair of *Tsaritsa* and the dispatching of other ships mean that he will have to remain on Sitka, but he still has to take us, and if we left him on Kodiak then he would be sick with worry and God knows when he would manage to return to Sitka. So we have decided to go directly to Kodiak and the neighboring islands from here, then sail around Kenai and Chugach bays and return to Sitka; we will drop Furuhjelm here, then we will go on to California. This will take us a total of about 10 days, but at least Furuhjelm will not worry, and things will go better for him.

Something strange has happened. After the captain of *Tsaritsa* left, the man with whom we sailed to Sitka, the ship was placed under the command of a man named Arkhimandritov. He is a very knowledgeable and experienced man, who has been sailing in these seas all of his life. Arkhimandritov was the skipper last year of the ship *Kadiak*, which he was given before Furuhjelm arrived in the colonies. He sailed many times on that ship, always successfully and safely. But suddenly something happened.

Near Kodiak Island there is a small island called Elovoi; a monk named Herman settled on that island some time ago; he was one of our first missionaries to the colonies. He lived there for a long time as a complete hermit. Then he organized a small school for Aleut orphans to whom he taught reading, writing and God's commandments. He died in 1837, was deeply revered by the Aleuts, and in his memory they built a chapel on Elovoi Island, near the place where he is buried. When Arkhimandritov sailed to Kodiak the first time, the wife of the former Chief Administrator, Voevodskii, told him that he should hold a memorial service in the chapel every year when he made his first trip. Arkhimandritov promised, but never carried it out. The first year he had successful sailing.

The second year he came to Kodiak again, took on a cargo of ice, and left for San Francisco. Several miles out of Kodiak, during ideal sailing conditions, on a clear day, 30 March of last year, his ship suddenly hit an unmarked rock. The damage was so bad that almost instantly water flooded the hold of the ship. The crew, officers and Arkhimandritov all saved themselves in small boats while the ship was adrift at sea for three days, kept afloat by the ice cargo. It finally drifted to Elovoi Island and sank directly in front of the chapel with just one mast above water, and a cross beam which looked like a cross. Was this chance, or a reminder from above? Judge it however you will but the fact remains. Since then Arkhimandritov has had no luck.

It is also interesting that when the ship took *Tsaritsa* in tow, it was early in the morning, and the day was clear and completely calm. Furuhjelm had come up to our rooms to watch *Tsaritsa* leave, since from our windows the entire harbor can be seen as if it were on the palm of your hand. He said his wife had just had a dream in which *Tsaritsa* was surrounded by a black cloud which was pushing her under the water. As he said this Furuhjelm was watching through the window with us. Suddenly we heard a shot, and then another, and then we realized that *Tsaritsa* was not emerging from behind the island where the ship had towed her. She was already grounded on a rock. Furuhjelm is a Lutheran, but all of this has affected him so much that he has resolved to give an icon to the chapel on Elovoi Island, and we have personally promised to offer memorial prayers when we reach Kodiak.

Our voyage promises to be successful. The steam clipper *Aleksandr II*, aboard which we are going to sail, is a fine ship and sails well, both under steam and under sail; she carries all necessities. We will not be sailing alone, which means it will not be monotonous, and the vast supply of provisions leads us to hope that we will not go hungry. Furthermore, Furuhjelm has already asked me to handle the general ship's business. And finally, we will be sailing during the best season of the year when there is neither fog nor prevailing strong winds. We would like to return to Sitka by Easter Sunday, but I do not know whether we can manage this. At any rate, we will remain on Sitka for three days and then go on to California. In all probability some of the ladies will accompany us. Our fine gentlemen [in Russia] should learn to travel like this; sometimes they cannot even manage to get to Kronshtadt, while here, it is considered nothing remarkable to sail 1,200 miles, which is more than 2,000 versts. And of course that is only one way; the return voyage is another 2,000 versts. for example, an 18-year-old girl, Mlle. Klinkovstrem, will sail to San Francisco with us. She has just become engaged to Furuhjelm's secretary, and since it is difficult to assemble a trousseau on Sitka, and her father and mother cannot leave New Arkhangel, she is going to San Francisco alone. She will live in the home of the Company agent there, buy the things she needs, and then return home. Fortunately the ship we are taking is going to return to Sitka, for the young lady had planned on traveling on *Tsaritsa* to California, staying there until another ship came, which would take her to Kodiak, and returning from Kodiak to New Arkhangel in October. Such trips are considered rather commonplace here.

The father and mother of this young girl are very distinguished people. Her father was formerly a valiant captain who served the Company for a long time commanding its ships. Then he was an agent in California, where he became an ardent Methodist. He is religious to the point of fanaticism, and honest in the fullest sense of the word. I liked him from the first moment I met him, and we have a very fine relationship, although we sometimes argue until we are exhausted. He bases his convictions on biblical texts, and I refute him with biblical texts. I am demonstrating to him that one can prove anything one wishes by quoting the Bible. Furuhjelm has an excellent English Bible, with commentary, and it is very often used. Basically I am trying to convince [Martin] Klinkovstrom that I would certainly convert him to Orthodoxy if only I had time to convince him. Speaking of Orthodoxy: one of the Kolosh toions is going to be baptized day after tomorrow. Kostlivtsov will be the godfather, and for that reason the Kolosh is going to wear (after the christening) a frockcoat with galloons of silver lace and trousers with a stripe down the side, and he will be treated to a dinner. Furuhjelm says that he could baptize all of them at once in the Kolosh River if he could declare that every baptized man would be given a blanket and two cups of vodka and a dinner. I am altogether certain of this, and he would do it, but one cannot expect anything of the present generation. This generation is lost, but future generations of Kolosh will not be the same.

I had intended to write just a few lines, but I was carried away and have written a whole page and still have not finished. It is already midnight, and too late to continue, so I will postpone the rest until later.

2/14 April 1861

Today I was present at two christenings. At 8:00 AM Kostlivtsov christened one of the Kolosh toions. This great lout was forcefully shoved into a large tub, and when he emerged from it, they put a cross on him. For a few moments he stood as if he were dazed, and not because of the cold water, because these people bathe in the sea in 10° of frost; he himself said he did not know what had happened, but he felt just as if he were drunk. After this, I attended Mass, which was performed by the Bishop, and then at noon after the service, I went to Furuhjelm's where the Bishop baptized his newborn son. Then there was a big dinner, at which even Madame Furuhjelm was present.

Tomorrow I am going to start packing my trunks. On Tuesday the people here are giving a big dinner for us in the club, and on Wednesday we will be hastening on our way toward Europe. I am grateful to everyone here, and especially to Furuhjelm, for all their kindness, but the urge to return home is very strong. Here it is just as if we were in some desert where the voice of educated persons is rarely heard. Since I have been living here and have become briefly familiar with everything, I have become convinced that the devil is not as frightful as he is painted, and if it were not for the isolation from the rest of the world, and the severe climate, then it would be possible to live here. All the same, thank God I do not have to . . .

Kodiak Island, Pavlovsk Harbor   12/24 April 1861

Well, here we are, and we have sailed 600 miles north, my dear Maman and chère soeur P., and we are now abiding on Kodiak Island, one of the most important in the Aleutian archipelago. I will begin from the time when I finished my last letter, which was sent from Sitka to California aboard the *Nakhimov*. On 5 April the New Arkhangel people gave a farewell dinner for us in the club. According to custom, they made *speeches*, drank toasts to our health, we responded, et cetera. On the 6th at 9:00 AM the *Aleksandr II* was completely ready to put out to sea. The wind was quite brisk, but it was with us, and in spite of the cold and rain, we decided not to postpone our departure, so that we could use the favorable wind to make as much mileage as possible that day. All the Sitka people were waiting for us at the harbor, including soldiers and laborers. We said *do svidaniia* to all, and precisely at 6:00 we had prayers aboard the ship, and at 9:45 we raised anchor. Everything went smoothly as we left the harbor, but then the wind changed, and it was so strong that the waves came from all sides. The ship was tossed about so unbearably that everyone became seasick, including Furuhjelm and not excluding me. I went to sleep at 3:00 in the afternoon and did not wake up until 9:00 the next morning. By then the wind had subsided enough so that we could raise the sails to help the engine and proceed in the proper direction. That day I was alone all the time, for the rest could not stir out of their bunks. On the 8th and 9th the wind was favorable, and although the ship was tossed about considerably, nevertheless my companions came back to life and emerged from their cabins.

At 11:00 AM on the 10th we entered Pavlovsk Harbor on Kodiak and the weather was beautiful and calm. We appeared here completely unheralded. They had expected us after Easter, and thus nothing had been prepared for our arrival. We took quarters in the home of the office administrator. Our arrival actually could not have been timed more perfectly. At Pavlovsk Harbor we met Aleuts from all over the whole department who had gathered here to go out on a sea otter hunt, so we were able to question them all, and talk with all of them. This really greatly facilitated our work and saved us the necessity of traveling aboard baidarkas to distant settlements where it would have been impossible to go by steamer because of all the rocks and the lack of harbors and docks. Our ship unloaded supplies here and sailed to Kenai Bay to take on a full load of coal while we are inspecting Kodiak. It will return here in several days, so we will not have to stop very long in Kenai. Once we have made our necessary inspection there we will hurry along, the sooner to return to Sitka and then be on our way to California.

There is nothing much to be said about Kodiak. It is a mountainous island of volcanic origin, as all the Aleutians are. In summer it is covered by dense green grass. There is very little forest here, and that only on one tip of the island, and on the nearby islands. There are whales in the bays and around the islands; these are the favorite food of the Aleuts.

The streams abound in fish from May to September, so that even the bears, of which there is no small number, catch them with their paws. According to native stories, a bear will squat down on his haunches in the river, up to his neck in water, and when the fish swim upstream in schools and approach him, he puts his front paws out in front of his chest and snatches several fish. Then he gets up tosses his catch on shore, and sits down again and fishes until he feels he has enough for his breakfast or dinner. Then he comes ashore and starts to eat, but he only eats the cheeks and leaves the rest. Local bears do not bother humans and livestock. We happened to see how they will go down to the little streams to drink right alongside the cows.

In addition to bears, there are many fox, arctic fox, halibut and other fish, as well as enormous crabs. The natives eat only the legs of these crabs, and each is as long as a man's arm. Yesterday at supper five of us could not finish the legs of one crab! All these fish, shellfish and animals represent food and wealth for the Aleuts. From all the evidence we have collected, and from the accounts of Aleuts themselves, with whom we talked for two days, here is what I can tell you about these people.

The Aleuts inhabit all the Aleutian Islands, the Alaska peninsula and part of the North American coast. They are divided into several tribes. On the mainland they have intermixed with local Indians and have lost their original identity and have taken the names of the places where they live, such as Kenai, Chugach, et cetera. The pure Aleuts are those who live on the islands and are called Atkhinsk, from the island of Atkha; Unalashkinsk, from the island of Unalaska; and Kadiaksk, from the island of Kodiak. formerly these were quite warlike people, who often fought among themselves with great ferocity. They used to be idol worshippers, and were, as it is officially expressed, *under the delusion of shamanism*.

Russian promyshlenniks who came to the Aleutian Islands at first lived on friendly terms with the natives, but then began to lord it over them as if they were in their own land. They stole the catch of furs from the Aleuts, insulted them, took their wives and daughters, and finally provoked the islanders beyond endurance. In one winter the Aleuts seized and burned three Russian ships that had wintered on the islands and killed the crews, thinking that they had forever rid themselves of their oppressors. But the following spring new promyshlenniks appeared, and when they learned the fate of their comrades, they took fierce vengeance on

132

New Arkhangel. The path along which Golovin and Kostlivtsov walked.

the Aleuts. The names of Glotov, Solovei and others are remembered by the Aleuts to the very present day. Whole settlements were destroyed, and neither women nor children were spared. There were no horrors beyond these monsters. With the establishment of the Russian American Company and the inspection of the colonies by Councillor Rezanov, everything was brought into order; but the population of the islands had already been decreased by half. Subsequently smallpox wiped out another large part, so that now no more than 5,000 or 6,000 persons remain. Of course it goes without saying that after such a debacle not a trace of warlike spirit was left among the Aleuts.

In appearance the Aleuts are small and awkward; the habit of spending most of their time from their early years on in a baidarka where they use only their arms, means that all their strength and agility is concentrated in the upper torso; the legs are crossed and motionless which causes the upper trunk of the body to develop but the legs to remain short and crooked. The result is that the Aleuts walk in a duck-like fashion, waddling from one side to the other. Their faces are swarthy and covered by coarse dark hair that grows very low on the forehead. They have narrow eyes and prominent cheekbones, so that they very much resemble the Kalmyks. But the women are not bad looking. Conversely, an Aleut man is really beautiful in a baidarka.

They are all Christians. The Gospels, catechism and a good many prayers have been translated into their language. They go to church very zealously and decorate the chapels with various things they bring in and fulfill all their duties. But we are told they do not have a genuine religious feeling. They do have a need to pray, it is true, but if they were told tomorrow that they must become Mohammedans, they would only ask why; if they were told that those were the orders, then without thinking, they would attend a mosque and perform *namaz** just as they presently go to church and light candles in front of an icon. By nature they are very peaceful, submissive and good. They patiently endure every

---

*Ancient muslim prayer. — Eds.

privation and are not selfish. They are quick to take offense even though they try to conceal this; they are lazy, carefree and gluttonous. In general, thievery and other minor misdemeanors do not exist among them. Quarrels are infrequent and always peacefully resolved. They love vodka, but they never drink to the point of falling over dead drunk or staggering.

They are governed by their toions whom they elect themselves. The toion only supervises public order and is responsible for the elderly and the orphans and the organization of hunting parties, but is not personally in command of them. All quarrels, discords and misdemeanors are resolved by the group as a whole. Since there are no crimes here, and no law suits or such problems, there is no court system, no police. Everything is resolved by general consensus. For misdemeanors arising from laziness, the Russian administrator has the right to reprimand the guilty party directly, or in the presence of the toion, and to order him to work for an extra day. But he is forbidden to hit him or to inflict corporal punishment, and indeed he dares not, for *an Aleut who has been punished like this will not go on living—he will either hang himself or throw himself into the sea.*

They have no obligations to the government. They do not pay soul taxes, have no quitrent obligation, are not recruited for military service. Their only obligation is to go out to hunt at the order of the Company, to catch and to sell their furs to the Company at an established price. Actually, this responsibility is not as burdensome as it may at first appear, and it is quite necessary. I have already mentioned that the Aleuts are exceptionally lazy, irresponsible and gluttonous. If an Aleut manages to prepare dried fish (iukola) for himself, and whale blubber, then he will lie down and eat until nothing is left. When he has finished up everything and hunger stirs him again, he will put out to sea to catch fish if the weather permits, or he will gather shellfish along the shore, and in the interior of the island he will gather roots of various plants and whatever berries may be ripe. If the weather is bad, and in fall and winter this is often the case, then he and his whole family will suffer famine and will have to exist on walrus or sea lion hides which he cuts up into bits and boils in sea water. Because of these propensities, it is necessary to force them to prepare extra supplies for themselves for winter, and to earn money so that they can purchase flour, fat and any necessary clothing. It is because of this that at a designated time the toions and other important Aleuts gather together in the main settlements and, at the request of the administrator, decide how many men from each settlement should be sent out that year to hunt sea otter; how many should carry on other types of hunting, so that enough workers remain at home to prepare fish, blubber and other food for all. When all of this has been decided, the prikashchik issues, *without charge*, to each settlement, everything they need to prepare their baidarkas: that is, lumber, poles, hides, whale sinew and whiskers, as well as all hunting weapons, including powder, shot, guns, et cetera. If an Aleut prepares his baidarka himself, he receives money fot it.

In April, when everything is ready, the parties are sent out to hunt in designated places, and all during that time they are maintained at Company expense. Upon their return the Aleuts give the furs and receive payment, at a set rate, for each pelt. Anyone who wishes to keep furs for his own use has the right to do so. When they receive the money for their furs, the Aleuts buy everything they need in the Company store, also at a set price. Meanwhile the Company hires women and young Aleuts to catch fish in streams and dry them, so there will be enough both for the free supply for hunting parties, and to sell the Aleuts in winter and spring when their own supplies are exhausted, for it frequently happens that in winter an Aleut will come to the prikashchik and declare that his belly is hungry and that he wants something to eat and has no money for provisions; then he will be given as much iukola and blubber as he needs, without cost.

If the Company hires an Aleut for a year or two and sends him to another island during that time, then it provides him with living quarters and food, and pays him an annual salary of 250 to 350 paper rubles. Of course orphans are cared for, and the old and infirm without families, all at Company expense. It appears that our colonies are the only place in the world where there is not a single beggar.

Thanks to the organization of schools and concern on the part of the administrators, a large part of the Aleuts know how to read and write, and in some places, on the islands of St. Paul and St. George, for example, *there is not one single illiterate person*. Generally speaking, we have not found any trace of the slavery or oppression about which we had heard so much in Russia. One can sooner reproach the company for overconcern, which has made the Aleuts too dependent on handouts and has made them even more irresponsible. As for the fair sex, one cannot say that these women are very chaste. Russians are much to blame for this, for they came to the islands and instilled in the Aleut women all sorts of nonsense and special rules so that these savages, who had very little conception of modesty, easily became subject to abuse by Russian promyshlenniks. They are very naive, and say they cannot refuse a man, cannot annoy him, when it is so simple and easy to satisfy his demands. Even the Aleut men have become accustomed to this order of things, and they are not at all concerned about any little infidelities on the part of their wives. So long as their households are cared for and the children are tended, the women may satisfy anyone they wish. Moreover, frequent famine during the winter months weakens the Aleuts, and when a man's belly is empty and his strength fails him, there is no thought or desire to have amorous relations with his wife, and therefore an Aleut makes no claims on her. If he finds a *polovinshchik* who will look after his wife so she will not be bored, and will help support the family with his own contributions, since some or perhaps all of the children may be his, then so be it. The local clergy is trying to change this situation by imposing penance, but this does not help the matter at all because local authorities do not find it necessary to interfere in the family affiars of the Aleuts. The polovinshchiks actually increase the population, and this is beneficial to the region.

Well, here you have a brief description of the Aleuts and their way of life. I hope that some privileges which we hope to secure for them will improve their situations, and when they become accustomed to caring for themselves, they will be happier and better off, although it is impossible to change their way of life completely because of the climatic conditions in the region, where nature itself has placed limits on the well-being of men.

This letter has been written in Kodiak, where I will continue it when I have some free time, and I will finish it in California, from where I will send it to you. Just now we are waiting for calm weather so we can go by baidarka to the neighboring islands to view the life of the Aleuts and the local settlers. It is impossible to go out when the seas are choppy since the voyages are very long, as much as six hours, and in a strong wind it can take up to twelve hours. Besides, it is not exactly comfortable sitting in a baidarka. You sit on the bottom, with your legs stretched out, and you have to remain in this position the whole time. Your legs and your back go to sleep, and you cannot move because the baidarka would turn over. Although you might not drown, you would have quite a bath, and a cold bath in April is not appealing. We are also going to choose a bride for an Aleut who lives on Sitka. You see, he has decided to get married, and there are no eligible women there, so he has asked us to choose an Aleut girl for him from any settlement, saying that he has complete confidence in our taste, and will marry with his eyes tightly closed. We will try to find someone and bring her with us to Sitka.

18/30 April 1861

We have spent all of these days traveling about in baidarkas, inspecting the nearby islands to see the life of the Aleuts and Russians and creoles who have settled there. I must confess that we have found that all of them, especially the settlers, live very well. It is true that the Aleuts live in little dwellings half buried in the ground, but this has always been their manner of building, and they prefer living like this to being in large light izba [cabin], which is considered altogether too roomy. As for the settlers, there is really nothing to report. They have large light homes with outbuildings, stockpens, gardens, et cetera. The interior walls in many homes are papered or are covered with sailcloth that has been decorated. Everywhere things are clean and pleasant. Nearly all the settlers, that is, those who have previously been in service to the Company, receive pensions which range from 150 to 700 paper rubles. Land and wood are given to them free of charge, as much as they wish. So that they can build and settle on the land, the Company makes a gift of either the necessary equipment and tools, or money, and often both. Each person who wishes may receive livestock with the understanding that after five years he will return the offspring or make a payment of money plus interest, figuring the value of a cow at 40 paper rubles.

With all of this it would seem that there would be no reason to complain, but there are still persons who ask either that their pensions be increased, even though they are doing absolutely nothing for the Company, or that their debts for livestock be canceled, trying to convince everyone that there was no off-spring, while upon actual investigation it is apparent that they all sell heifers on the side for quite a profit. In short, in chatting with the Aleuts, and in fact with all the natives, we have come to the conclusion that they are not in slavery to the Company at all, but that in fact the Company itself has become a slave to them. How the Company is going to extricate itself from this situation God only knows, for it will be no simple task to change all of this.

We have now completed our inspection of the local area, and will go on farther as soon as our ship appears. It is time, because we are finally becoming bored with seeing and hearing the same thing over and over again. We have found a wife for the Sitka Aleut and are bringing her with us. We have also been to the chapel of *Herman*. On the same island where the chapel is located we visited a settler, an elderly man of 70. He says that God's punishment has befallen him and his family. His elder son drowned; the daugher of his second son, who is now 12 years old, was born without hands and feet; his elder daughter's husband is paralyzed and has been bedridden for seven years. The sight of the small girl with no hands is very tragic, although she is not bad looking, and her black braids are simply beautiful.

In good weather travel in a baidarka is quite comfortable. You lie as if you were in a cradle, rocking from one side to the other a little, and eventually you become drowsy. Of course for long trips it is very tiring to sit like that, but there is no avoiding it, everyone has to get used to it. And when it is rough, then you get splashed, or rather, your head gets splashed, because the rest of your body is enclosd in the baidarka; right up to your neck you are tied into the craft with a special drawstring which keeps water from getting into the baidarka; but the waves wander through your hair, which is nothing, except that your eyes are full of salt water.

28 April/10 May 1861

Well, here we are back on Sitka, which looks just as it did when we left. However, we have been gone for 21 days, and during that time we have gone more than 1,500 Italian miles, under sails and steam, and we managed to inspect everything. Now I will continue where I left off.

After we had inspected Kodiak and the nearby islands, we took the ship to Kenai Bay, which we reached on the 21st, after our noon dinner. I left Kostlivtsov to inspect the coal mines and went on by ship farther into the interior of the Bay for about 70 miles, to a place where there is a redoubt and the Kenais live. We reached that place at dawn the next day, and I immediately went ashore. I inspected the awesome redoubt, which would require several old women armed with oven forks to capture. I then went through the forest to the Kenai settlement. The day was clear, and it seemed too hot to wear a coat, so I took it off and hung it up in the forest on the first fir tree I came to. Furuhjelm followed my example and we went on.

The Kenais live in a poorer condition than the Aleuts, but by contrast they are more vivacious. By their clothing it is apparent that they are hunters of land animals, and they very much remind me of the Indians whom we had an opportunity to see in paintings. They have long hair worn the way our women do, tied in a heavy knot on the back of the head. This hair style and a shirt made out of animal skins (a *parka*), make it difficult to tell by appearance whether a person is a young boy or a woman. I was very surprised when one toion introduced his family to me and said these were his sons, when I had been certain they were his daughters. I talked with people in their izbas and asked the Kenais about their needs and their requests, and then I returned to the ship, picking up my coat on the way, which I found just where I had left it.

On the morning of the 22nd I was at the coal mines where Kostlivtsov was awaiting me. I looked at the mines myself, and at all the buildings, and questioned the soldiers and the service persons. Then we continued our journey.

We were at sea on Easter Sunday. At midnight the whole crew gathered in our cabin, the captain read the prayers and then together we sang "Christ has risen" and exchanged Easter greetings. Then we ate *paskha* [Easter cake], and went to bed. Sunday night, when you were celebrating the first day of the holidays in St. Petersburg, the wind came up, and was ferocious until early morning. For a long time I could not go to sleep, and twice I was almost pitched out of my bunk, and all that time I was thinking about you and about what you are doing while I am gone . . . and I became very melancholy. At the very time when all who are dear to my heart are approaching this glorious holy day within our family circle, here we are sailing alone in a far distant inhospitable region. The dark night, the foaming sea, the cold wind howling in the shrouds—our ship creaks in every joint and is tossed from one side to the other by the waves—in a word, there is little poetry and much yearning. And under the bow of the ship there are rocks both below and above the water, some charted, and some unknown!

Toward the morning the wind subsided. We started the engine and proceeded toward Nuchek Island where there is a Company redoubt, as well as some Chugach settlements. At 9:00 AM we dropped anchor in a vast bay well protected from the sea. The administrator of the redoubt came out in a baidarka, wondering why a ship would come so early in the year; he was completely dumbfounded when we told him that we were officials who had come from St. Petersburg to inspect his redoubt. After we had talked to him, we went ashore.

The redoubt is exactly the same as the one in Kenai Bay. All the Chugach poured out of their huts to meet us. We went into one hut and jumped back out as if we were on fire, so dreadful was the stench of fish. One more minute and literally I would have been violently sick. But the Chugach are not at all bothered by this smell, and in fact they are permeated with it. After we were out in the fresh air we gathered all of the Chugach around us, explaining the purpose of our visit, and asked them to let us know if they had any requests or complaints. Their requests were limited to the fact that they would like to have an increase in pay for the work they do for the Company. *Currently they receive 40 paper kopecks per day, and they would like to receive 50*. Of course we promised to take this up with the Governing Board. Soon thereafter one of the crowd began to speak with unusual zeal and gesticulation, and the whole group began to accompany him. By the expressions on their faces and their gestures, it was clear they were very dissatisfied with something. When they had stopped shouting, we asked the interpreter what they wanted, and he replied that they had heard that the administrator of the redoubt might be replaced, and they were declaring that they were very much pleased with him, that he was very good to them, and that if he were replaced, they would all immediately go off into the interior of the country and not heed anyone else who might be sent. We replied that there had been no talk of replacing the administrator, and that since they were satisfied with him, no one would trouble him for a long time. You should have seen how glad they were. They bowed and shouted to express their complete satisfaction.

This administrator was appointed by the Company about 10 years ago. He is a simple Russian peasant, no longer young, but he is literate and very intelligent. Of course we thanked him for his fine administration, which was best attested to by the general love for him on the part of the natives around there, and the fact that the service personnel of the redoubt, all of whom had been asked if they had any complaints, had all responded that they were well pleased and could not wish for a better administrator. We left a supply of rum, flour, butter, sugar and tea in the redoubt, and also various small trade goods for the savages. I ordered that each, without exception, be given vodka and tea. We then left to go out to the ship; in about two hours we raised anchor, and with a favorable wind and good weather, with sails raised and engine operating, we made our way to Sitka. We arrived here at 8:30 last evening, making from 10 to 11.5 knots per hour the last day, which is between 17.5 and 20 versts per hour.

They had not expected us on Sitka before the 5th or 6th of May at the earliest, and so they were very surprised when they saw our ship. Madame Furuhjelm immediately ordered that our rooms be warmed and had supper ready for us, and the whole population of Sitka came to the harbor to meet us. After we had eaten supper we of course retired, and I snored like 99 bagpipes, it was so pleasant to rest in a warm room where I was not being pitched out of my bunk by the waves and having a headache from the pounding of the screw.

The first thing this morning the Bishop came to see us to greet us upon our arrival, and he visited for more than an hour. We could not give him any good news about the missions under his jurisdiction. Then the office administrator appeared. He is a very good fellow, and he asked us to take his dear wife to California with us. She is a very heavy woman, not old, but she is a nervous German, and on top of that she is suffering from some imaginary ailment. The wife of our captain will also sail with us, and the fiancée of the local secretary. Several others also asked to sail with us, but we refused these requests because of the shortage of space. I still cannot say for certain when we will leave. We have completed all our assignments, but when our ship was sailing to Kenai for coal, it hit a rock, and although there is neither visible damage nor any leaking, and although we all managed to reach Sitka aboard her, nevertheless Furuhjelm is afraid to send her off to California without a preliminary inspection, and for that purpose it will be necessary to unload her and bring her up on shore. All of this will take at least a week. There is nothing we can do about it except just wait. Today we have already taken our walk into the forest, and tomorrow I will start to put into a report form my impressions during the last part of my journey.

2/14 May 1861

Our ship was hauled up on shore, inspected, and no damage found, so she is quite ready today. If circumstances permit, then we will set out on our return voyage after our noon dinner tomorrow. And it is high time! I am certainly hoping to find your letters in San Francisco. I will have to rest a little and refresh my thoughts, because my head is literally splitting, what with all the Aleuts, the Kolosh and the creoles. All day, from morning until night, I hear nothing but talk about Company matters, so that even in my sleep I dream of various accounts, reports, petitions and other such business. I would like to reach California and not have to wait too long for a ship, because there is no special entertainment in San Francisco, although generally speaking there is a great deal of interesting activity in America . . . but this will all be as God wills!

San Francisco   11/23 May 1861

Here we are, back in California, and this time we made the trip from Sitka in eight and a half days. Actually, we left Sitka according to plan, with good weather, and in spite of the wretched cargo of coal which we were carrying, we proceeded well, and today at 4:00 AM we dropped anchor in San Francisco harbor. To our dismay we did not find any letters from you. Kostlivtsov received just one, dated in February, in which his wife wrote that all of our letters were being sent to the Amur [River], and this means I will not have any news from you until I reach New York, where we expect to be in about 30 days. We reached here just after a ship left, so we will have to wait eight days for the next one. We rented quarters for one dollar per day each, very clean rooms in the home of a French woman who was recommended to us by Madame Laguarde, who you may remember traveled with us from New York to California. You should have seen how delighted this lady and her daughter were when we came to them! An elderly man, Gr., another of our old acquaintances, also had us at his home for several hours.

You have probably heard that there is civil war here in America, but our journey lies away from the theater of war and thus will be completely safe. Besides, there are naval vessels to convoy the passenger ships, so we can sleep peacefully, which I hope to do, if the tropical heat does not prevent me. I want to reach New York as soon as possible, then when we finish our business with the envoy, we will proceed on to Europe where the political situation is changing so rapidly. I am sending this letter by overland post, and will hurry to finish it in order to send it off tomorrow morning. I thank God for good health and I hope we will finish our business in good conscience so that neither the Company nor the government will have any cause to reproach us. We left the Sitka people as friends.

Steamer *Orizaba*, in the Pacific Ocean   22 May/3 June 1861

I am beginning this letter en route from California to Panama, and I will send it off to you, my dear Maman and soeur P., immediately upon my arrival in New York. By that time you will already have received my letter from San Francisco, which I sent from there via the so-called *Pony Express*. This is a special type of post which operates overland all the way from San Francisco to St.

Louis with unusual speed, using small horses called *ponies*. From St. Louis it goes on by rail, so that a month and a half after the day a letter is sent from San Francisco, it can be received in St. Petersburg. I have already written you that thanks to the thoughtfulness of the [Russian] American Company, all of our letters have been sent to the Amur, so we will not receive them until we return to Russia.

When we came to San Francisco, we naturally went to see the consul, and then we visited our old acquaintances, every one of whom received us with open arms. We did not want to stay with the consul because he had so many guests, and so we decided to stay in an inn, but everything we looked at seemed quite dirty. Fortunately while we were searching for quarters we called on Madame Laguarde, and when she discovered our problem, she immediately recommended Madame Parrin to us; she keeps a small hotel and rents quarters only on the recommendation of persons she knows very well. Madame Parrin gave us two clean rooms for a very reasonable price, and we immediately moved into our new quarters. Madame Parrin has just one son and one daughter, both grown, and both very well mannered. The daughter is about 17 and is quite attractive and very well brought up. I will tell you a story about this young lady which again testifies to my scatter-brained condition, which Pierre of course will be delighted to hear about.

One evening when we returned home I stayed for a rather long time with Kostlivtsov, whose room is just below mine. Finally the time came to retire, and I went up to my room. The light had gone out on the stairway and Kostlivtsov wanted to light my way, but I said I didn't need a light and up I went. My door was the third on the upper floor, and when I had left it, I did not lock it with the key. So there I was in the dark, going up the stairs, groping for my door, opening it, and entering. It was dark in the room, as I had expected, but in vain I searched in the middle of the room for the table where I always have a candle and matches. I looked all around, but the table was not there. Some other person would have realized immediately that he had entered the wrong room, but I stood in the middle of the room, thinking God only knows what, and asked myself what had happened to that table? At that moment, beside me, I heard the voice of the daughter of the hostess who was murmuring something in her sleep. You can well imagine that I beat a hasty retreat, and this time I found my own door. It happened that the door of the daughter's room was just beside mine, and I had entered thinking I was going into my own room. And on top of this, the next morning when I was washing, I thought of something I wanted to tell my servant, who was brushing clothes in the corridor, so I opened the door and was talking with him; as usual without thinking, I went out into the corridor in a very *skimpy* costume, and just then the daughter of the hostess came out of her room. Well, what an embarrassing situation! But in spite of all these little incidents, it was fine living there.

Thanks to the generous hospitality of our acquaintances, time passed rather quickly. Thus on 14/26 May, a Sunday, a man named Mora Moss, about whom I probably wrote to you during our first stay in San Francisco, invited us to his home for breakfast. He has a dacha about 10 miles outside San Francisco in the hills. At 10:30 AM we boarded a steamer which took us to the other side of the bay, to the little town of Oakland, where Moss was waiting for us with horses, and we drove along a beautiful road which has been planted along both sides for a long way with strawberry beds. By noon we reached Moss' house and immediately sat down at the table. There were four of us, Moss, his lady friend who lives with him, *maritalement*, Kostlivtsov and I. Breakfast was marvelous, with every possible delicacy. At 4:30 in the afternoon we returned to San Francisco. Madame Laguarde's husband was waiting for us at the harbor, and he invited us to dine with them. In spite of the fact that we were very full, it would have been impolite to refuse, because they do not have any free time except Sundays. We sat down at the table at 6:00, and dinner ended at 11:00 that evening. I must tell you that Laguarde is just a gunsmith, but here the class of master craftsmen consists primarily of very fine people who are working to save money to return to their homelands.

All officials such as senators and others belong to the class of persons called *politicians*, and are concerned only with how to secure administrative positions and to seize profit from the treasury and from the people. Compared to these gentlemen, our Russian grafters are simply innocent children.

This is how we lived in San Francisco until our ship, *Orizaba*, was ready to leave. We have quite good accommodations on her, and thanks to the efforts of our friends, Captain Pearson is doing everything possible to see that we are comfortable. As you might suppose, we have already made the acquaintance of most of the first class passengers. The food is fine, especially since the captain has assigned a special man to us, a Frenchman, with instructions to care for our comfort at all times. We are sailing quite well, but it is still rather cold and the sun has not yet broken through. However we are not sorry about this, because there will be plenty of heat later. I cannot say much yet about our present group. I will write later, when I have come to know them better; for the moment, I will say only that there are not many passengers, and the main thing is that there are very few children. At least our ears are not aching and our heads do not throb from shrieks. This letter is being written very poorly because although I do have a place to write, the steamer is vibrating so much that the pen is jumping around as if it were in a mortar.

Aboard *Ariel*,
in the Gulf of Mexico   8/20 June 1861

Seventeen days have gone by since I started to write this letter, and already the major part of our voyage to New York has been accomplished. Everything went very well, except that rain followed us constantly. Captain Pearson was thinking about our comfort right up to the last day. We became acquainted with almost all the passengers, and time passed quite rapidly, but as before, the heat overpowered us.

On 3/15 June we reached Panama at 4:00 AM, and after a light breakfast we took a small ship and went quickly to the city. A train was ready and waiting for us. Kostlivtsov and I put the luggage we had with us on our shoulders and ran, so we could get seats in the railroad car. We managed to do this, but when we put our luggage in the car and took our places I was almost literally dying from heat and thirst. I assumed the train would stay for another quarter of an hour until they had loaded the baggage and mail, so I stepped out of the car to look for something to drink. I had just gone a few steps when the whistle blew and the train began to pull out. I thought this was a false warning and that after it had gone a few feet it would stop, but this was not the case. The train began to pick up speed, so that I had to run to catch up with the car, and I made a running jump into it as it moved by. Back home I would probably have been left behind because the conductors and other officials would not have let me run and jump into a moving car. But here no one pays any attention to you. Everyone minds his own affairs, and if you should happen to fall under the car, well, that is your own problem. So I found myself in the car and thirst continued to plague me. I walked out to the observation platform where several other passengers were standing. One of them who had seen me running and jumping onto the train noticed that I was mopping my brow with a handkerchief and using it to fan myself, and he quietly pulled a cup out of one pocket of his coat, and a bottle of cognac from another pocket, and gave them to me. I confess that it was with great delight that I took several swallows. Right after that another gentleman gave me a bottle of ale, and a third passenger offered me oranges, and a fourth, two eggs. So I had a little breakfast right then and there. When I had finished this, I smoked a cigar and spent the whole time out on that little platform chatting with the passengers.

At 9:30 we reached Aspinwall, where *Ariel* was awaiting us. We boarded at 1:00 PM, and at 2:00 we pulled out of the harbor and

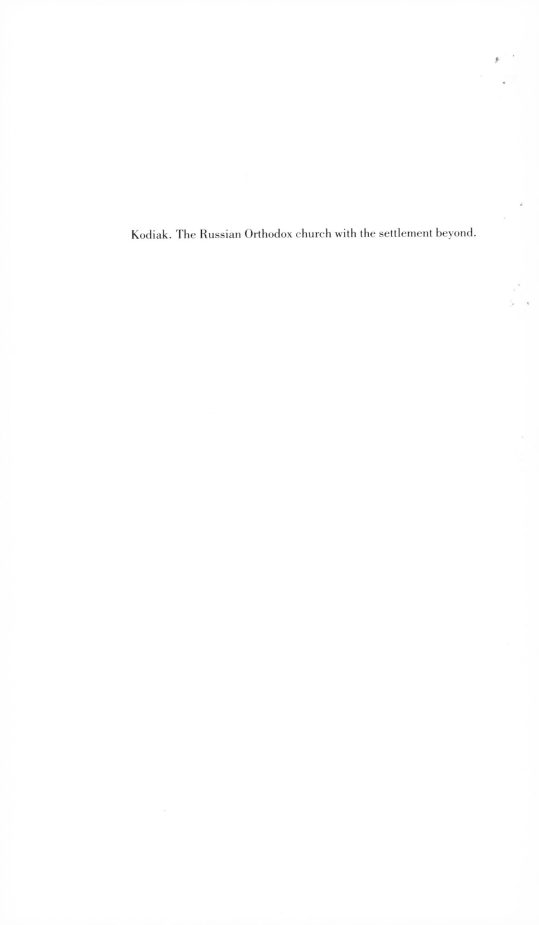

Kodiak. The Russian Orthodox church with the settlement beyond.

proceeded along our way. We had letters of introduction from San Francisco to Captain Wilson, and he immediately took us to the largest and quietest cabin on the whole ship, assigned a special servant to us, and asked us to let him know right away if there were anything we needed. Thus everything is fine, and it is quiet for us aboard *Ariel*. The Antilles met us inhospitably; the wind was steady and strong, with frequent squalls, thunder almost every night, and it was still hot. We are sailing well, and I hope that we will be in New York by Monday, 24 June. I will finish this letter there, because it is almost impossible to write aboard this ship, since it is so very rough that everything slides off the table. On to New York.

New York   13/25 June 1861

Well, here we are at last in New York. Yesterday noon *Ariel* brought us to the capital of the United States, as the Americans themselves call New York. Of course the first matter of business was to send a messenger to Lobach and Sheppeler, to find out whether there were any letters for us. After an hour, Schultz, the office manager, came to us and brought me your letter begun on the 17th and completed on the 30th of March. Although much time has elapsed since that letter was written, I was nonetheless very much pleased to receive it. You see, I have not had any news from you since October, because the [Russian] American company decided to send all letters addressed to us to the Amur, where they will sit until next year.

Tomorrow night we are going to Washington, and will probably stay there three or four days. Then I would very much like to take the steamer *Africa*, which is leaving here next Wednesday, 21 June/3 July. But God knows, will we manage to do that? *Africa* goes to Liverpool, and from there it will take three or four days to Paris, with appropriate stops.

You have probably either read or heard that a civil war has broken out here in America. With the election of the new president, who belongs to the party who want to free the negroes, the southern states, whose prosperity is based on negro labor, broke away from the Union and resolved to organize a separate federation. The northern states, adhering literally to the Constitution, do not recognize this separation, and have resolved to use force to compel the southern states to remain in the Union. Both sides have armed, and there have already been several battles. At any moment a decisive battle is expected in Virginia. But there is no need for alarm here. The Union army controls all transport between New York and Washington, and rail travel is open and quite safe.

It is reported that the southern states have armed several privateers in order to intercept commercial vessels belonging to the north, especially ships that voyage from San Francisco to New York, since those ships always carry a large amount of gold. Therefore both *Orizaba* and *Ariel* were outfitted with cannon and carbines, and all the passengers including me were provided with revolvers. Every ship that came over the horizon was taken for a privateer, but to the disappointment of a considerable number of passengers who wanted to fight, and to the great relief of the captains of the ships, we did not see a single privateer, and we reached New York in the most peaceful manner possible.

We are staying in the Prescott House on Broadway, in the best part of the city. Our rooms are good, the cuisine is European, and we pay 2.50 silver rubles each, for two rooms, breakfast, lunch, dinner and supper. Furthermore the entire staff speaks German and French, and is much more helpful than in American hotels.

Yesterday for the first time after a 23–day fast we ate well. The food on American ships is generally poor, and aboard *Ariel* it was simply dreadful. By the end of the voyage I had stomach pains. Americans do not seem to mind it; they have absolutely no conception of good food, and they *devour* every abomination with the same gusto. They do not like to change plates, but eat everything from the same one. After the soup they have a roast, then fish with a sauce. A young lady sat across from me who consumed an unbelievable amount of various things, especially white beans, which she ate with horseradish, pepper and vinegar, washing everything down with tea. All Americans eat ham with syrup! The devil only knows what kind of palate they have, but they certainly do not understand good taste.

When we reached New York we almost had a problem. When we left St. Petersburg, they issued us only enough money for half a year, and the Company was instructed to give us the rest upon our request. Well, the Company gave us promissory notes on the banking house of Brandt and Company in London. The house of Brandt was so well known that promissory notes on it are willingly accepted everywhere. We had already exchanged such notes in London, New York and California; then, when we left California, we exchanged one note to pay for our trip, and kept several dollars so as not to have to carry gold, assuming that when we reached New York we could exchange another one. Imagine our astonishment when we were informed that Brandt had declared bankruptcy, and that those notes were not being accepted anywhere. We were absolutely penniless! Fortunately Lobach and Sheppeler told us they would give us as much money as we needed, not on Brandt's notes, but just on a straight note with a transfer of this debt to the Company. So we have managed to solve this problem. After I have finished this letter I will go to Lobach and receive my share, which is 5,000 francs, or 1,250 silver rubles, which will be enough for me to reach St. Petersburg.

What more shall I tell you about myself? I am healthy, thank God, and will write to you from Paris or London, because once this letter is sent, I will be leaving for Europe in just a few days. On this trip there is no need to fear privateers, because we will be traveling on either an English or a French ship, and anyone harming the English or the French would bring real trouble on himself. So please do not think about any possible dangers for us, and be calm while you are waiting for my letter from Europe. Until then, goodbye . . .

After I had sent my letter from New York, we stayed in that city for two more days, and on Thursday the 27th, at 7:00 AM, we left on a special train to Washington. We did not ride, but almost flew, and therefore the whole trip took only 10 hours. There are military forces stationed everywhere all along the road, either in towns or villages or in camps. But the trains move freely, and no one anywhere asks passengers for passports or identification, so everyone carries on just as in peacetime. In Washington there are now about 60,000 persons. Part of these are militia, that is, mobilized national guard, and although these men are no good as soldiers, at least they behave themselves.

The same cannot be said about the American volunteer troops. They are riffraff gathered from everywhere, from factories and workshops, who have abandoned all pretense of working. They are unskilled laborers from large cities, and some are just barely out of prison. This free-wheeling enterprise elects its own officers and does as it pleases, staggering about the taverns from morning until night. These men stop pedestrians asking for money, and since they all have a revolver or a knife in their belts, it is understandable that a pedestrian would be foolish to refuse, especially at night on deserted streets. They even break into homes. Our Minister, Stoeckl, went out one evening with his wife to go to a party, and left just one old houseman at home. Suddenly three armed soldiers came in and went right into the room. The houseman asked them what they wanted. "We want something," replied the soldiers, "and we will certainly get it. Are you all alone in the house?" The houseman ran to the window and started to shout to other people, although he knew very well that no one else was at home. His ruse worked well. The soldiers were afraid they would be apprehended, and ran off.

Everything is dreadfully confused. No one knows anything. Everyone is afraid of treason. Soldiers even spread a rumor that the water wells and fountains had been poisoned. Every moment one regiment or another is mutinying. And they all go free, because no one dares lay a hand on a soldier. Sometimes they even shoot peaceful citizens who are so ill-advised as to go near a camp. Just yesterday a little girl about six years old stopped near a camp at about 3:00 in the afternoon to have a drink of water from a fountain. A sentry shouted at her twice, and since she did not understand that he was speaking to her, she went on drinking. The sentry shot her, wounding her in the arm, and they had to amputate the poor child's arm above the elbow. The sentry justified· his action by saying that he only wanted to frighten the child, and had fired accidentally, not knowing the gun was loaded! What kind of soldier is that?

Military operations have still not begun, but from time to time there are skirmishes in the advance positions, or more precisely, an enemy who is familiar with all the trails will try to steal through the advance posts of the Union armies almost every night, and he will kill as many sentires as he can. Because of this, 12 to 15 men are killed every day. Inexperienced officers also help the enemy a good deal.

One general who had been promoted to that rank from being an attorney, went by rail with 500 men on reconnaissance. Sitting in a car, His Excellency probably forgot the purpose of his journey, or perhaps he was dreaming that he was proceeding like a peaceful citizen to plead some case. His dreams were interrupted in the most unpleasant way: the train ran straight into the fire of enemy batteries, which destroyed the rail cars and killed or wounded the majority of soldiers aboard. The general himself was wounded and barely managed to avoid being captured. The rest of his command fled into the forest, and one by one the men reached camp however they could. They were not pursued because there were only about 50 men in the battery. It costs the government a million dollars a day to maintain such forces (1,300,000 silver rubles)!

Yesterday we had dinner with Stoeckl, and he is coming to see us this morning. I believe we will finish our business tomorrow, so on Monday we will go to New York. We already have tickets for the steamer *Bremen* which sails on 6 July for Le Havre.

Well, the journey to Washington ended successfully. While we were there we had dinner with Stoeckl twice, and he came to spend three hours with us. During these meetings we completed all our business with him. He is in complete agreement with our ideas and will write accordingly to the Grand Prince [Constantine] and to Prince Gorchakov. In short, so far, everything has gone well; but when we reach St. Petersburg, we will have a great deal to argue about, not only with the Company, but also with certain persons who have heard from various sources about the colonies but have not the slightest understanding about the situation, who confuse the Kolosh natives with Aleuts and creoles, who base their opinions on theories, possibilities and rumors; or to be more direct, on the testimony of vocal persons who for one reason or another are dissatisfied with the Company, beginning with my associate Ppv., who in an article he wrote for *Morskoi Sbornik* made many mistakes. Fortunately our conclusions will be based on facts, not on assumptions. The resolution of the problem will take considerable time, if everything is to be done which will benefit both the country and its population, and not be detrimental to the government. If this is resolved too quickly, it is doubtful that any good will come of it. From a distance many things seem different from the way they look close up; in the case of the colonies one must be right there in order to judge properly and not make a mistake which will be difficult to correct. We will do everything conscience dictates, but as the proverb goes, I am an outsider. If they do not accept our arguments, we will wash our hands of the affair. However in this regard I have full confidence in the Grand Prince, who always acts for the common good, and will not want the whole country to suffer from haste or from the prejudices of a few persons.

We left Washington yesterday morning at 7:00. We had scarcely taken our seats on the train, pleased with our choice, when a drunken soldier came into the car and sat down right next to me and after a few minutes began to snore, leaning on my shoulder. Of course I jostled him and shouted into his ear at the top of my voice that he could go to the devil, but he snored on dead to the world, so I just took him by the collar and pushed his head over to the other side. He woke up a couple of hours later, got up, and since there was an empty bench behind Kostlivtsov, the soldier stretched out on it by the window. After a few stations two more young soldiers got on, also feeling merry, and sat down next to us. Soon one got into conversation with his companion who passed him a canteen of spirits, and both of them began to drink until they had drained it. Finally all three became drunk and went to sleep, one on Kostlivtsov's shoulder, and the first one who had been sitting behind Kostlivtsov stretched out on the bench with his feet against Kostlivtsov's back. We shook them and shouted at them, but in vain; they only mumbled in their sleep without stirring, and it was impossible to move them. Against our will we had to wait for them to wake up. Finally in Philadelphia they did wake up, and left.

We reached New York at 8:00 PM and stayed in the same hotel. They had our rooms ready for us, and all our belongings were in place. We have our tickets for *Bremen*, which leaves here Saturday, 6 July. Since a ship is leaving tomorrow, I am taking this opportunity to send this present letter to you.

We looked over the ship today. Our quarters are fine, and they say that the food is good. There is a grand piano in the main saloon. The ship is sailing to Southampton, England, in nine or ten days, and there they will immediately transfer us to a small ship which will take us to Le Havre. The cost is $100 each, which is 133 silver rubles, for the passage from New York to Le Havre. We are very glad that we will soon be off. In the first place, when we reach Europe we will be almost home, and in the second place, dollars fly away here like swept dust. Just for example, one journey to Washington cost each of us more than $60. Under such circumstances one cannot economize on his expenses, rather, only be concerned with how to make ends meet.

Tomorrow we are dining with our banker, Sheppeler, and with his first assistant, the prikashchick Sh., whose brother serves in our Navy and whose wife is Russian. Thursday evening we will go to visit Sh., and in the afternoon we will watch various processions and demonstrations from our balcony. That day is a holiday commemorating the anniversary of the Constitution of the United States. But now it is time to put this letter in the post. I hope to be home by August in any event. Now, on to Paris . . .

New York   22 June/4 July 1861

The ship on which my last letter was sent, my dear Maman and soeur, left New York yesterday noon; today I am starting another letter to you which I intend to mail from either Le Havre or Paris. These are all excerpts from my travel notes, all intended to be a conversation by correspondence with you.

This is how I have spent the last two days. Yesterday morning I strolled through New York looking at the city; among other places I went to the Museum of Barnum, the greatest charlatan in the world, who became famous through his memoirs in which he very openly tells how he has hoodwinked both the Old and New Worlds. In Europe he exhibited the famous dwarf, Tom Thumb; in America he made money from Jenny Lind. It is interesting now to see his museum, which has the only living *siuch*, a family of albinos, and a creature which is neither human nor monkey—the devil only knows what it is. In appearance it is a young negro without hair on his body; although the head and arms and legs are formed like those of a monkey, and they are hairless also. The creature cannot speak, but seems happy in spite of the fact that it has a most melancholic expression. Along the way we stopped to look at sewing machines of all makes, types and appearances; we finally asked our banker, Sheppeler, to buy a sewing machine for each of us and to send them to St. Petersburg on a ship which sails in August and will be in St. Petersburg in September. Then at 6:00 PM Sheppeler called for us and took us to have dinner in one of the best local restaurants. We had a really superb dinner. Everything was so delicious and so plentiful, but because I did not take the precaution of eating just a little of each thing, I had to just nibble at a superbly delectable dish of snipe, served roasted, which I am very fond of, and I had to leave the grapes, raspberries, cherries and pineapples almost untouched. We left the table at 9:30 and I went for a stroll along the streets to see how people were celebrating.

Today, the Fourth of July, is celebrated here as the day of the declaration of the federal constitution, or rather, the declaration of personal freedom to every citizen. At the present time, when the Union is already on the verge of breaking up, and civil war has already begun, the Fourth of July is celebrated here with the same exultation and noise as usual. It is a holiday for every citizen, a holiday of freedom. As a result, ever since last evening my head is splitting with the unaccustomed noise. On all the streets, in the shops, and on the boats, they sell fireworks. Not only every single child but even many of the adults amuse themselves by tossing these into the streets—little firecrackers, rockets and roman candles. They fire off their guns and revolvers and pistols—all to celebrate freedom. All last evening several ladies who live opposite our hotel amused themselves by tossing roman candles onto our balcony, and they stopped that game only when one candle fell into our sitting room through the open balcony door.

Our accommodations are very fine. We have two bedrooms and a huge sitting room, which is lighted in the evening by a gas lustre with 12 brackets. There is also a gas lustre in the bedroom, with eight arms. The sitting room looks out on Broadway, the best street in the city. We have soft furniture, velvet coverlets, mirrors, marble—it couldn't be more luxurious. And for all of this the two of us pay $6.00 per day (about 8 silver rubles), which includes breakfast, lunch, dinner and supper; the service is very good, and we have every possible comfort. You must agree that this is not expensive. In any other hotel we would have had to pay at least twice as much. In Washington we were fleeced mercilessly. For our three day stay we had to pay $40 (about 55 silver rubles) for two small rooms and a sitting room, and all were dark with an abundance of flies and mosquitoes that stung us almost into unconsciousness. And in contrast here there are no flies, no mosquitoes; the rooms are airy; the food is excellent.

The Germans are great lovers of titles and therefore they have elevated us to Princes, and they call us such things as *Altesse*, and are forever waiting on us. We are not spoiling their fun, but we have taken measures so they won't charge us extra for this princely service. So we are living very well. This morning all the troops in New York paraded ceremoniously down our street. We watched them, sitting on the balcony smoking cigars, according to the American custom, with our feet up on the railing. Both cavalry and infantry were in the parade, and behind them were crowds of youngsters dressed as zouaves, with all sorts of weaponry. Last year I saw young boys pretending to be zouaves, and I told Kostlivtsov that playing at soldier would not bring any good to the Americans. Now just a few months later all the states are on military footing, the military element predominates, the strong party wants war, no matter what may happen, and the military administration will use dictatorial methods to arrest anyone who even in the slightest disagrees with the view of the ultra Republicans. America was a good land, and to this very moment I am trying to understand how it could have happened that a nation could move ahead so rapidly and so well, when they do not have an orderly form of government, because everything is based on bribery and theft, starting with the President. Was this problem solved by the Constitution of 1779? Truly, this demands a great deal of thought.

This evening we are thinking about going to a park outside of town, because it is too noisy here. There are going to be as many as 15 displays of fireworks in the city, not counting rockets and other things with which young America is making do. On the 3rd of July a remarkable comet appeared, which none of the astronomers had even dreamed existed. The people look on it as a portent of disaster, and this could come true if the disagreements are not ended peacefully. Today we packed our personal belongings and will send them to the ship tomorrow. At noon on Saturday we will raise anchor, and 10 days later we will be in Le Havre. It is six or seven hours by rail from there to Paris. I am healthy as always, in better health than I was in St. Petersburg and on Sitka. My stomach bothered me considerably on Sitka to the point where it made me nauseated just to look at the wild goat. It is true that the food was bad on the ships, especially on *Ariel*, but during that time I lived on sea air. By contrast the air here is good, and the food is delicious and we sleep well in wide beds. In a word, everything is grand.

23 June/5 July 1861

At last the fireworks and the noise are over, although our ears could still use a little rest, because there is plenty of noise here from the constant traffic. I mentioned to you earlier that the windows of our sitting room face Broadway. Yesterday when the movement of carriages was much less than usual because crowds of people had been going out of town from morning on, we counted how many carriages passed under our window. In 10 minutes we counted 73. There is no doubt that on a usual day there would probably have been half again as many. Because we did not have anything to do, we went to one of the *Cafes chantants*, of which there are many here, but even there the place was full of the reek of gunpowder which had come in from the street.

The celebrations ended with a fire in one of the outlying parts of the city, but there was no great damage. I watched how the firemen rushed off to the place, carrying their fine fire equipment with them. They do not use horses here to power fire wagons; all the fire fighting equipment is steam-powered, and works wonderfully. It is a real pleasure to watch them. Some of the best people in the city serve as volunteer firemen. They serve for the glory of it, convinced that no one ever works as hard under the lash.

Judging by a telegraphic dispatch which came in this morning, things were bad in Baltimore. About 100 homes burned down, but that fire was believed to have been set by an arsonist. A large part of the population of Baltimore are secessionists, that is, persons who subscribe to the idea of breaking up the Union. Not long ago the military administration there arrested the head of the police, who was suspected of treason, and they replaced all the policemen. This is the reason they think secessionists may have deliberately set the town afire to demonstrate that with the change of policemen elected by the city there will be no order or security.

I went to bed at 1:00 AM, and slept like a corpse, since the fireworks had subsided by then. On regular days anyone who fires a shot on the street is fined $20. Today we received our passports with visas for Paris, and the money we need for the trip. We sent our personal effects off to the ship and now we are quite ready for our voyage. Tomorrow noon, God willing, we will be on our way.

Aboard *Bremen*, in the Atlantic   25 June/7 July 1861

Well, at last we left New York at noon today, and we have already come 250 miles from the *Imperial City*, as the Americans call New York. In fact, it really is imperial! What buildings! What wealth! What commercial activity and feverish motion everywhere! "Forward, forward!" This is the motto of the Americans. They really have gone ahead with gigantic steps. Because of this it is sad to realize that a civil war will immediately half this enormous activity which up until now has been based on commerce and industry, and will take things in a ruinous direction that will destroy all the good. In his last message to Congress on July 4, President Lincoln pointed out the necessity to act decisively, with armed force, to reunite the separated states to the federation. He asked for an army of 450,000 men and $400 million for that war, and he will receive it. But when will this civil war end? What will be the result of forcefully reuniting the seceded states to the Union?

Trade is being halted. The southern states' harbors are under close blockade, and they cannot find markets for their goods. They are contracting loans for the war and maintaining an army of 80,000 troops, but they are not paying anyone one kopeck. Payment will be made in better times, but for now, enthusiasm is supposed to support each and every one. However it is possible not to pay salaries to the volunteers who join the ranks of the defenders of their states; they are doing this not only from dedication, but also to save their homes and families from enemy invasion. But even an army of volunteers must be armed and supplied with food and clothing, and this is all very costly. Likewise the northern states are being forced to close factories and dismiss workers, since they are no longer receiving cotton and other raw materials from the South. They have had to impose new taxes on imported goods and resort to domestic loans to cover expenditures for the maintenance of the army. Even last September currency bills, that is, notes on various banks, were a rarity in New York, and everywhere transactions wre being conducted only in gold and silver. Now, although hard currency is still abundant in circulation, nonetheless the currency bills are appearing in very significant numbers, and almost any time you change gold money you receive paper in exchange. This war may deal a severe blow to freedom, a blow which will echo not only in America.

But enough of this. I will tell you how we left New York. On Saturday, July 6, I arose quite early in order to pack the last things without having to hurry, and so as to be ready to leave on time for the ship. The bill which the proprietor submitted to us seemed altogether reasonable. Then the proprietor, Dietz, sent our things to the ship with the head waiter, and we left the hotel at 10:30 AM, accompanied by the proprietor and his entire staff, who showered us with endless *Your Excellencies, Altesse,* et cetera. Upon reaching the ship we found that all our things had already been placed in our cabin, and our headwaiter was standing by, along with the ship's purser and the steward who will take care of our cabin. They greeted us with the deepest of bows, which deepened even more when the banker Sheppeler came to be with us. At noon all was ready, and at 12:30 we left the harbor to the shouts of "Hurrah!" from the whole crowd. Two salutes fired from the ship announced our departure from New York.

Bremen is a screw steamer of 700 horsepower which sails beautifully and is wonderfully built. Everywhere it is spacious, clean and orderly. The cabin we have is fine, but the ship's head waiter told us that there is an empty cabin for four persons next to ours, and that we may have it if we wish, without paying anything extra for all the additional space. He said that both he and the entire crew are at Our Excellencies' full disposal. The Captain in his turn also invited us to take the large cabin, and since on a voyage the first consideration is for comfort, and since we have had bad accommodations more than once this past year, this time we did not stand on ceremony. We thanked the Captain and moved into the large cabin. Dinner was served at 4:00 PM. Place cards indicated that we were to sit right next to the Captain. On one was written *Prince Kokchinoff*, which is Kostlivtsov's family name; and on the other, *Count Golovin*. We protested against the use of these titles, but they do not believe us and are convinced that we are traveling incognito. We even went so far as to show them our passports, to no effect. People look at them, smile knowingly and nod, as if to say, "Oh, yes, everything is in order. This is to be expected. Such important people do not use real passports." In vexation I wore my oldest jacket, but people are not at all dismayed. "Why shouldn't His Excellency wear an old jacket if he likes it!"

Aside from all the "Excellencies" and the bowing and scraping, everything is excellent. The cuisine is very, very good, in the French tradition. The manager of the buffet served as a chef at the Court of Darmstadt and knows his business. Everything is most deliciously prepared. At 8:00 AM tea, coffee and various things are served; at 12:00, breakfast; at 4:00, dinner; and at 8:00 PM, again tea and other refreshments. All of this is included in the sum of $100 which we paid for the voyage. The wine is very good and inexpensive.

We are sailing very well, but today the fog has been coming in ever since morning, and it is damp up on deck and a little too cold for someone who has just come in from the tropics. As far as the passengers are concerned, I must admit that they are not the most brilliant. The Jewish element predominates. However we struck up an acquaintance with some persons, including the Bishop of Cincinnati, with whom I converse partly in English and partly in French.

29 June/11 July 1861

It is five days since we left New York, and by yesterday we had completed more than one-third of our voyage to Southhampton, the English port from where we will be transferred to Le Havre on a small ship. So far our sailing has been exceptionally pleasant. The sea has been very calm with a light wind astern which helps the engine. The only unpleasant thing is the prevailing fog, which is usually to be found here at this time of year, which makes it impossible to be on deck very long. Nevertheless I do go on deck as often as possible, and only go below when my clothes are damp and I am chilly. Today the cold is quite pronounced, especially for those who not long ago were broiling in the tropics. Today we are sailing through the area where icebergs can be found, but we are not expecting to see any, because by this time of year they should be farther south. However in spite of this, all precautions are being taken not to run into one, especially in the fog; if we did hit one, sailing at a speed of 11.5 knots, it would be like running into an underwater rock.

When you receive this letter, we will be peacefully relaxing in Paris, and you won't have to worry about my tales. Time is going rather quickly for me, thanks to my having become acquainted with some of the passengers, particularly the Bishop of Cincinnati. I have someone to talk to, and I have been busy reading lately, which is very pleasant, thanks to the well-equipped main saloon and good lighting in the evening.

It is true that the children bother me a little sometimes; it appears that there are more of them than I had hoped, including four infants and half a dozen older screechers, but at least they shout in the saloon only from 8:00 in the morning until 8:00 in the evening. One can escape from them by going up on deck or into the smoking room. They are somewhat better supervised because their mothers are Germans, rather than Americans. There are also quite a few Jews sailing with us, but for the most part they are traveling in second class and are not in our saloon. Tomorrow it will be exactly one year since we left St. Petersburg, and what have we not seen in that time! Sometimes the days dragged on slowly and it seemed as if we would never come to the end of our tribulations. But looking back, the year has gone by, and here we are, almost with one foot in Europe! . . .

4/16 July 1861

Thank God our trip, or at least our sailing, is successfully coming to an end. We have gone 2,682 Italian miles, which is almost 4,700 versts, and now we have only 431 Italian miles to go to reach Southhampton, which will take just over a day and a half. Unfortunately, no matter how we count, we will still come into port after the departure of the ship which was to have taken us to Le Havre, so we will have to wait over in Southhampton a day and a half, which means a waste of time and money. In order not to delay this letter, I am going to send it on our ship to Bremen, and from there it should reach you in 10 days, so you will have information about me two or three days earlier. When I arrive in Paris I hope to find your letters there; when I receive them I will reply. The trip from Southhampton to Le Havre takes eight or ten hours depending on the weather, and it is six hours by rail from Le Havre to Paris.

What shall I tell you about our journey? Comfort and good food are prime necessities for a passenger, and in this respect we cannot complain. The food is splendid, our cabin is large and our linens are changed every day. I certainly cannot criticize anything having to do with comfort, service and good meals. On the contrary, everything is splendid. We are sailing very well—it is no joke to make an average of 300 miles per day!

In short, everything would be wonderful if it were not for the children! What a punishment to hound me for my entire voyage! I can accommodate myself to bad food, to poor quarters; but children—they are worse than any nightmare, worse than mosquitoes, worse than bedbugs. There were 60 of them on *Washington*. Here, about a dozen all told, but even that is enough to make me lose all patience. They wake up early, and first the three infants scream; one of these is a gruesome little creature which very much resembles a monkey. At 8:00 AM all the rest appear, and the pleasure of their dear little company continues until 9:00 PM. It would be nice if they took turns shouting, but they do not. One hungry little girl usually starts the concert out of courtesy and drags out an unbearable note; then in an instant all the rest take up the harmony, from eight months to seven years old, inclusive. The infants are not long behind, and thus they create such music that one's ears split and the head spins. The little young mothers smile prettily and frantically kiss their dear little children. Do you remember how you used to be deafened by the heart-rending shrieks of the hordes of parrots and peacocks and the screaming of the monkeys when we used to go to the zoo? Well, there is some similarity between that and the concert we hear every day. It would help if one could escape by going on deck, but this is impossible when the fog and rain force one to sit in the saloon. Fortunately there is not much time left to revel in this.

God willing, tomorrow night we will be in Southhampton. I will finish this letter as soon as we reach port and will give it to the Captain to be sent to the proper quarter. As for me—thank God, I am in good health.

5/17 July 1861

Today at 9:30 AM we finally sighted the *foggy shores of perfidious Albion*. At this very moment we are passing Lizard Point, which means that we will be in Southhampton between 2:00 and 3:00 AM. We will be in Europe! In honor of this joyous occasion we are going to have a bottle of champagne at dinner, and I must admit that I will toast the European shores from the bottom of my heart.

Yesterday we sailed very well. The weather was excellent, especially in the evening, so that I spent almost the entire time on deck chatting with the passengers, and especially with the Bishop of Cincinnati, who is a worldly and very interesting man. He told me that several years ago in Belgium he had given the last rites to a famous criminal prior to his execution. The Bishop came to Europe at the very time when the crime was being recounted in all the papers. A young count, with the aid of his wife, had killed her brother in order to acquire his property. The Bishop said:

I do not know why it seemed to be that God had chosen me to be the confessor for this criminal, and to provide guidance for that last moment. I had been in Rome, in Vienna and in France, and everywhere I was haunted by this idea. Finally I went to Belgium, where I learned that the trial was over, and that in spite of the efforts of relatives who had strong influence at court, the young count had been sentenced to death, and that the execution was to be performed the next day. I immediately went to the prison, but they told me I had to have permission from the Prosecutor General in order to meet with the criminal, and that anyway the criminal had declared that he did not wish to see any priest, unless it might be a hermit priest. There was nothing to be done, so I walked away from the prison to return home, but half way home a young man caught up with me and said that the Prosecutor

General would let me see the criminal and wanted me to return. When I entered the cell of the accused count, he met me coldly, asking who I was and what I wanted. I introduced myself and said I had come to hear his confession and to prepare him for the final moment. The count listened to me and said he was ready to accept my services. I remained with him all day and all night until the following morning. In my presence the executioner cut off the collar of his shirt and tied his hands. Then we were put into a cart and set out for the place of execution. The mayor of the town stood at the foot of the guillotine. I went up on the platform holding and comforting the criminal. When his head was placed on the block, he kissed the cross, and his last words were, "Sainte Marie, mère de Dieu, priez pour moi . . ." and his head rolled onto the platform. When I stepped down and looked at the mayor of the town, I had to tell him how pale he was. "If you were to look at yourself," he answered, "you would also be surprised that you too are as pale as death." And just then a peculiar emotion seized me, and to this very day, when I remember it, I hear the deafening sound of the falling axe.

That is just one of the many very fascinating stories the Bishop told me. In this way, in conversation and in reading, time has gone rather quickly. But all the same, it is time to be home.

Paris   7/19 July 1861

The moment I arrived in Paris I sent a man to the post office to see if there were any letters for me, and an hour later I had your letters, my dear Maman and soeur P., dated June 9–10. So I know that a month ago you were both in good health, thank God. I hope that now with the summer air your health is good, and also that everything at home is well.

In reference to my trip, I will add to the letter I sent you through *Bremen*, that we arrived at Southhampton 6/18 July at 4:00 AM. A small ship took us in to shore right away, because *Bremen* does not go into the harbor there, but stands at anchor at Cowes on the Isle of Wight. I must tell you that the ship from Southhampton to Le Havre only sails on Mondays, Wednesdays and Fridays, at 11:30 PM, and since we arrived on a Thursday morning, this meant that we would have to wait almost two days in Southhampton. How vexing! we thought, and with foresight we set out for the steamship company to tell them that if we had to stay there two days it was going to be expensive, and was there no other way to get to Le Havre, since we had already paid for ticket? Was there any way to solve this problem? The agents talked together and told us that if we wished, they would refund our money for the trip to Le Havre. Fine! we said, and when we received the money, without stopping very long to think, we went right to the railroad station. "Two tickets to Brighton, please." At 6:00 PM we were in Brighton, and there took tickets directly to Paris through New Haven and Dieppe. At 9:00 PM we reached New Haven; at 11:00 we were sleeping as if we were in a bivouac, aboard a small ship which rolled so fearfully that almost all the passengers were lying in front of the basins; at 5:30 AM we arrived in Dieppe in one piece, no worse for the wear. We showed our passports and again went to the railroad station, then on to Paris, where we arrived at 1:00 PM. By 2:00 I was sitting in the bathtub washing off all the dirt of the journey. Don't you agree that it is not bad to reach Paris on the 13th day after leaving New York? It would have been even sooner if it had not been for the fog, which delayed us a good deal, especially at night.

Well, here we are in Europe, almost home. As I look back I almost can't believe how in the deuce we got to 60° of northern latitude, into that impenetrable remote corner of the world, as guests of savages. It all seems like a dream, difficult at times, and on other occasions full of interest and diversity. We are staying here in the same hotel where we were before.

Yesterday we went to say farewell to the *Bal Mabille*. What a charming little place it is! The garden is not large, but the lighting, the plantings, the flowerbeds are all done in superb taste. In spite of the fact that some loose women such as Mlle. Rigolboche, and the elderly Chicard gentleman whom we saw yesterday, dance the cancan with too much enthusiasm, Mabille is not like a tavern, as our country places are, but rather, everything is quite proper and orderly. Quite distinguished people come here to enjoy the eccentric dances. Actually, even the most conservative person would not shock people by saying he had been in the Bal Mabille. I also went to the *Comedie Francaise* and saw the famous Samson, the best of the local actors, whom I liked immensely. We also went to the *Palais de Justice*, where we saw a public trial. In short, we go everywhere where there is anything of interest to see and to hear. Today we plan to go to a new Russian church which is to be completed soon, and from there to the *Palais de l'Industrie*.

The weather continues to be good, in general, and although it occasionally rains in the morning, this does not inconvenience us, but on the contrary it serves to make the air fresh and lays the dust. I must say the streets here are very well kept up. The road, the macadam, as it is called, is so well paved that it makes a smooth and completely even surface, as if it had been covered with asphalt. You walk in the middle of the street as if you were walking on the best exceptionally well-paved sidewalk, and the amount of traffic is not less than on the Nevskii Prospekt at the busiest time of day.

Well, here you have a brief description of our life in Paris. I will give you all the details when we are together again, for these stories will take a long time to tell. For now, I will finish this letter so as not to delay mailing it. You have probably already received my letters from New York and from Bremen and even from Paris.

And so, *do svidaniia* . . .

INDEX

Reval (Tallinn, Estonia), 83
Rezanov, Nikolai P., 133
Rhine (river), 12, 13
Riddell (captain), 79
Rimskii-Korsakov, Nikolai
   Andreevich, 1n
Rimskii-Korsakov, Voin
   Andreevich, 1n, 103
Rosseau, Jean-Jacques, 18
Royal Gardens (Berlin), 3
Rue de Rivoli (Paris), 30
Rumeiro, Don Pedro de, 57
Russia, 93, 110n
Russian American Co., 6, 7, 63,
   73, 75, 79, 84, 85, 92,
   100-103, 117, 125, 126, 128,
   133-35, 138, 140, 141, 143-45,
   149, 151, 154
Russians, 11, 41, 81, 85, 88, 89,
   94, 96-98, 107, 108, 136, 137

Sacramento River (U.S.), 64-65
Ste. Chapelle (Paris), 18
St. George (Alaska), 136
St. Louis (Missouri), 144, 145
St. Nicholas' Day, 91
St. Paul (Alaska), 136
St. Paul's Cathedral (London), 29
St. Petersburg, 1, 20n, 42, 145
St. Ursula (church, Cologne), 13
San Antonio (California), 71
San Francisco, 62-65, 69, 71,
   75-79, 143-46
Sans Souci (Germany), 5
Santa Ana, Antonio Lopez de, 58
Seine (river, France), 23, 26
Serebriannikov Bay (Alaska), 124
Severnaia Pchela (Russian
   periodical), 10
Sewing machines, 66, 67, 156
Siberia, 75
Sitka (Alaska), 63, 64, 75, 76,

78-80, 85, 86, 89, 90, 92, 93,
   95, 100, 105, 106, 111, 114,
   118-20, 124-26, 128, 130, 139,
   142-44
   see also New Arkhangel
Slavery, 40, 74
Solovei [Solovev] (promyshlennik),
   107, 133
Southhampton (England), 168
Stephenson (ship), 53, 59
Stettin (Germany) 1, 2
Stewart's Store (NYC), 39
Stock Exchange (London), 29
Stoeckl, Édouard de, 43-46, 48,
   152-54
Surly Man, The (play), 110
Swinemünde (Germany), 1

Telegraph, 78
Terry, David S., 71
Thames (river, England), 29
Theatre, Concerts, Drama
   see specific works or composers
Théatre de Palais Royale (Paris), 20
Théatre des Varietés (Paris), 22
Théatre du Vaudeville (Paris), 28
Thumb, Tom (Charles S. Straton),
   156
Toions, 95-97, 134
Tower of London, 29
Traviata, La (opera by Verdi), 45
Tremont House (Boston), 35, 36
Trône, Place du (Paris), 23
Trovatore, Il (opera by Verdi), 40, 74
Tsaritsa (ship) 63, 64, 74, 78, 79,
   109, 112, 125-28

Uglichaninov (prikaschik), 93, 94
Unalaska (Alaska), 93, 132
Unalashkinsk Aleuts, 132
United States, 36, 65, 66, 74, 149,
   150, 157, 159-61